*A CHOICE OF*

ENGLISH

*ROMANTIC*

POETRY

EDITED WITH AN INTRODUCTION BY

*STEPHEN SPENDER*

---

*A CHOICE OF*

# ENGLISH

*ROMANTIC*

# POETRY

Granger Index Reprint Series

BOOKS FOR LIBRARIES PRESS
FREEPORT, NEW YORK

STANDARD BOOK NUMBER:
8369-6064-5

LIBRARY OF CONGRESS CATALOG CARD NUMBER:
71-80379

MANUFACTURED
BY
HALLMARK LITHOGRAPHERS, INC.
IN THE U.S.A.

# A CHOICE OF
# ENGLISH *Romantic* POETRY

[3

# CONTENTS

# CONTENTS

[5

# CONTENTS

# PREFACE

ROMANTIC is an idea irremediably vague by reason of the vagueness of the experiences it describes. Used in the most general way, it suggests a setting or scene, which in its turn suggests atmosphere. Forests, cliffs, mountains, torrents, caves, icebergs, the opened emptiness of expanses of sea or of plains, the horror of moonlit graveyards: such scenes of vastness or of solitude suggest the true romantic setting. But the romantic solitude is an inhabited solitude, a civilized solitude, a communicable solitude, almost a voluble solitude. It is the solitude of the Ancient Mariner, which has entered into his bones, burns from his eyes, and preys on the listener. The inhuman, fierce, untamed jungle or desert, the vastness of the scientific universe expressed in measurements which cannot be grasped as expressions realizable by the imagination, are even more alien to the romantic than to the classic temperament. The romantic landscape is a garden in which the flowers are allowed to grow wild; and in the early nineteenth century it grows side by side with the "classical" eighteenth-century garden, which itself may include a grotto, a cave, a torrent—some deliberate romantic effects. If we set ourselves the task of looking for nineteenth-century romantic features in English poetry, we soon must count Young's *Night Thoughts*, Blair's *Grave*, Gray's bardic primitives, Ossian, Burns, even Pope's *Windsor Forest*.

If a romantic setting and mood make romanticism, then these

# PREFACE

are permanent aspects of poetry. Keats, looking for ancestors, found them in Chaucer, Spenser, the Shakespeare of *A Midsummer Night's Dream*, and certainly in Milton. If to be romantic is to be violent, desperate, strange, farfetched, isolated and perverse, then Webster and Tourneur out-romanticize *The Cenci* and *The Prisoner of Chillon*.

Yet there is a difference between romanticism of the early nineteenth century and of other periods. Romanticism only expresses one mood of Chaucer, Spenser, Shakespeare and Milton who have other and profounder moods. If the later Elizabethans write in that manner of being hysterically out of sympathy with the society of their time which we associate with the Romantics, nevertheless their fury has an impersonal quality lacking in Byron, Shelley and Keats. Nor do they find that identity of their own moods with the mood of nature which we associate with the Romantics.

Perhaps the most striking feature of the poets of the Romantic Movement is their attitude to nature. The solitude of real nature is alien, immeasurable, inhuman; the romantic solitude is a vision of nature which reflects the solitude of the poet. The Romantic finds everywhere in nature his own image. This has the effect of spiritualizing nature whilst at the same time it makes his mind appear to have a kinship with landscapes, moons and vast waters. The romantic attitude, by the exercise of an audacious selectivity—which does not appear selective simply because the vast scenes chosen give the impression that the poet is one with the whole of nature—makes the natural scene which is outside the poet appear as a quality of his mind. What is peculiar and special about the poetry of the Romantic Movement is that outwardness so often takes the form of inwardness. I do not regard Barnes, Burns, Campbell, Clare, Crabbe, Gray, Hunt, Lamb,

Landor, Praed as true Romantics, because this transformation of nature into a quality of the poet's inner mind does not take place in their poetry, where nature retains its outsideness.

It would be crude to say that the romantic poets were simply egoistic and narcissistic. But in them or through them, the poet's isolated sensibility takes an egoistic form which sets up tremendous claims: of intuitive understanding and oneness with nature, in Wordsworth; of the "unacknowledged legislator" of mankind, in Shelley; of the poet devoted to "poesy" with a power of imagination enabling him to achieve complete self-realization in a world created by the imagination, in Keats; of a tragic poetic gesture which is its own justification, in Byron. In Coleridge, the romantic isolation is a divine and inspired weakness, a gift which asserts itself against the poet's conscious will, the weakness which the romantic artist of great objectivity and critical detachment must sadly admit to be a part of his personality.

The romantic in Shakespeare, Spenser and Milton remained always something on the outer edge of their poetic sensibility, the inner depths of which are deeply centered in other realities. Romance in them is a mood, a play to fancy. It is the dim background to a mysterious landscape in the foreground of which there is always the sense of the reality of the world with its secular and its divine institutions. Such poetry measures itself against standards which are not exclusively poetic. One might argue that the poetry of Shakespeare's most romantic plays was the purest he wrote, but not that it was the greatest. For the greatest is the poetry of the tragedies, which is great by being measured against the subjects of which he wrote; and these are great by the same standards as we measure the greatness of gods, kings and men with a living greatness of flesh and blood, heaven and earth.

At the back of the Romantic Movement is the idea that poetry creates its own kind of reality, a world of the imagination realer than the real world (in Keats) or capable of transforming it by a kind of chemical action moving outwards from the imagination until finally it affects the shape of society (Shelley) or by a fusion by a shaping mind in nature with the shaping mind of man (Wordsworth). This could only lead logically to a condition of affairs where life and society are judged by the standards of poetry, instead of poetry judged by them. The events that happen in such poetry, as a consequence, have a poetic importance which is different from the importance of events in the world. If there is a world of poetry, more valid than the actual world, there is no reason why in such a world a king should be more significant than a beggar or a murder be more tragic than any lesser episode of life. Or if the events of the world are reflected in such poetry, they assume a poetic significance which may be parallel with their significance in the real world, but which is not the same. Because of this romantic tendency to create an interior world of poetry, we do not care about the events in the narratives of Shelley and Keats in the way that we care about those in Chaucer and in Spenser. It is not just that Shelley and Keats create an unreal, fairy world; but they create one in which there is no necessary connection between its values and those of the real world.

Keats is not the most self-dramatizing of the romantic poets, yet he is the one in whom the romantic tendency to regard the aim of poetry as the creation of an interior world more satisfactory than the real world is most often expressed. The very fact that in real life he was a commonsensical person makes him state his romantic aims in a matter-of-fact way: "Now it appears to me that almost any man may like the spider spin from his own inwards his own airy citadel—the points of leaves and twigs on which the spider begins her work are few, and she fills the air with a beautiful circuiting. Man should be content with a few points to tip with the fine Web of his Soul, and weave a tapestry empyrean—full of symbols for his spiritual eye, of softness for his spiritual touch, of space for his wandering, of distinctness for his luxury."

He set out in his poetry to create this world where the poet who had renounced worldly ambition, opinion and certitude of faith, makes for his soul and even perhaps for his body a dwelling where the senses can delight themselves through the power of imagination. At first, in his letters and his poetic epistles, this idea has about it the insistence of affectation. At all events, his poetic world at this stage is not full and complete enough to convince the reader. In these Epistles to his brothers and his friends he is led on from line to line, from rhyme to rhyme, as by a fairy chain with links of poetic association.

> Just like that bird am I in loss of time,
> Whene'er I venture on the sea of rhyme;
> With shattered boat, oar snapt, and canvass rent,
> I slowly sail, scarce knowing my intent;
> Still scooping up the water with my fingers,
> In which a trembling diamond never lingers.

Here one rhyme suggests another, and that other suggests an image which is always chosen for its poetic quality. There is a luxury of poeticization in the early Keats. Yet this method is not the "free association," practised by certain modernist poets. "Free association" is the adoption of a sequence of the first words, ideas or rhymes which come into the writer's head, without his exercising any conscious principle of selection. Keats undoubtedly did have a method of selection. He himself would have called his principle "Beauty," and he would have said in his rhyming he followed where Beauty led. There is intensity in this free, wandering, purposeless pursuit of an undefinable objective. Heaping delight on delight, he arrives somewhere, perhaps at a glimpse more charming than those preceding it, or perhaps merely, as it were, at the edge of a cliff or in the center of a little wood. His early poems give often the impression of taking the reader for a gentle walk through groves and shrubs in the midst of which one catches sight of a nymph or a goddess. He justifies writing the long poem *Endymion* as "a week's stroll for the summer."

He is greatly preoccupied with the idea of the poet and of "poesie." The poet for him is neither prophet nor dreamer: he is the holder of the key to a garden of delights for which the real world can willingly be foregone. But it is undoubtedly in the Odes that he gives us the completest vision of a self-sufficient world of the imagination. These poems are felt to be unique in English poetry, yet it is difficult to put a finger on the secret of their uniqueness. What, though, immediately strikes one is the completeness with which each contains its own mood. Each Ode is a picture, harmonious, painted in fresh and natural colors with warmth and detail and supplied with a frame shutting it off from everything else. Each attracts the utmost sensuous satisfaction from the contemplation of a scene, a mood or an object. The strength of these poems lies in their quietness which separates an autumn day, an evening scented in the branches of a tree, a Grecian urn, the mood of tenderness and love, in all their naturalness, from the world and transforms them into the world of purest poetry. The Odes are dwelling houses of pure sensation equipped with every facility which can delight the spirit and the body:

> . . . in the midst of this wide quietness
> A rosy sanctuary will I dress
> With the wreathed trellis of a working brain,
>    With buds, and bells, and stars without a name,
> With all the gardener Fancy e'er could feign,
>    Who, breeding flowers, will never breed the same:
> And there shall be for thee all soft delight
>    That shadowy thought can win,
> A bright torch, and a casement ope at night,
>    To let the warm love in!

The Odes are offered as substitutes for the world, but it is the sense that the world which is drawn into them as ripeness is absorbed into the fruit of a peach, drawn in and then shut out, which gives them their deeply concealed drama. In the *Ode to a Nightingale* the world, with all its anguish, haunts the distance; and we scarcely know whether the song of the nightingale is the silver key which locks us into a magic box or whether it opens a dreadful reality "Where youth grows pale, and spectre-thin, and dies."

Keats comes nearest to expressing the philosophy of his poetry in the famous lines which are in themselves a characteristic example of the collapse which occurs when the romantic poet attempts statement of the kind which should be as true in prose as in poetry:

> "Beauty is truth, truth beauty," that is all
>    Ye know on earth, and all ye need to know.

What these lines mean is, simply, that poetry is all we need on earth. They are an audacious way of stating that poetry can create a world truer than the world of reality.

# PREFACE

The purpose of this Ode is to make the imagination enter completely into the scene created by the Grecian artist, where a lover is:

> For ever warm, and still to be enjoyed,
> For ever panting, and for ever young.

Keats breathes life into the scene depicted on the side of the Urn and in exchange he partakes of its immortality. The Urn has become a habitation, a symbol of fulfillment, a "friend to man." In this poem the poetry has as subject a "thing of beauty" the Urn itself, which might be equally the poem itself, that "sense of Beauty," which "obliterates all consideration." If poetry can create a reality realer than life, then to say that "beauty is truth, truth beauty," means something in such a world: and there is a special force in the exhortation "that is all, ye know on earth," which points to art as a way of life.

Romanticism is not absolute. It is a tendency away from an external type of poetry towards one in which external nature appears to become part of the inner consciousness of the poet, whilst poetic sensibility becomes the hidden center, delivering its veiled judgments, secretly adjudicating. The unromantic tendency is poetry as an instrument of language interpreting nature and a system of values, a voice which can perhaps make mortal flesh immortal but which always remains separate from the object (or perhaps I should say the subject-matter) of the poem.

With unromantic poetry, the difference between the real and the unreal, between fancy and imagination, between subject-matter and language, are as apparent as that between woodlands and a mountain range. In the world of romantic poetry there is a more blurred distinction between what is real and what is unreal, because everything is soaked in the poetic. The fairyland of Keats and of Shelley has a less clear significance than that of Spenser or of Shakespeare. Of course Keats and Shelley no more believe in the actual existence of their fairylands than does Shakespeare believe in Oberon and Titania. But their fairies are not just fancies. What they do believe in is the power of the creative imagination to invoke an ideal world: and in this ideal world everything imagined is a means by which the poet lives his life into his poetry. The power of being able to imagine what is unreal is already to Keats a kind of reality, because the imagination is itself the realest power in living: and the power to imagine what might be real is to Shelley a way of investing one's spirit in a future where the poet's imaginings will become a social and political reality.

The Romantics emphasize one aspect of imagination: inventive fantasy. They lack the imaginative power which has a firm grasp of objectivity and of systems of thought. As Keats (who of all these poets understood best the implications of the romantic position) noted, Wordsworth when he becomes sententious, Coleridge when he is pious, and Shelley when he is politically doctrinaire, collapse in their characteristic ways, which are familiar to readers of their poetry. Yet it is not sententiousness, piety, and political opinion which cause these collapses, so much as the failure of the poets to express their prose thoughts in their poetry. It is of the very nature of romantic poetry that it cannot reconcile itself with prose. If Byron succeeds in *Don Juan* in being a politic commentator and a social satirist, here he is least romantic and most near to Pope and Dryden, the models whom he really admired. Byron's romantically dramatic personality in his poetry misleads us into forgetting that of these poets he was the one furthest from the romantic spirit: his one great romantic achievement was the transformation of his own personality and behavior into a poetic romantic legend where they are safe from the judgment of the moralists.

Many readers today will assume that there is an irreconcilable antagonism between the poetic and the prosaic. This is because they have been brought up in a romantic and post-romantic tradition. They forget how easily Shakespeare moves from poetry to prose, how many of the speeches of his plays, which do not jar with the poetic passages, are simply prose passages lifted from Plutarch or some other source and rhythmed to fit into the scene. They forget how much of English poetry up to the nineteenth century expresses thoughts equally true as poetry or prose. This easy transition from the poetic to the prosaic was due to the fact that both uses of language were concerned with material which existed outside the language, as flesh and blood or a system of ideas.

But romanticism is the tendency to regard the material of poetry itself as poetic. Romantic poetry allows none of its content to remain itself. It melts everything down into an interior flow of romantic imaginings and then it recreates everything in a world of poetry removed from the standards of actuality. Coleridge, who was a Romantic in spite of himself, tried to correct the self-sufficiency and independence from conscious judgments of his own poetic thought by introducing a moral purpose into many of his poems. The effect is to blight the organic, spontaneous and original development of a dozen poems with what appears to be a Black Frost of Christian thought.

Once again it is Keats who expresses the romantic view in his famous theory of Negative Capability: "when a man is capable of being in uncertainties, mysteries, doubts, without any irritable reaching after fact and reason. Coleridge, for instance, he goes on to say, "would let go on a fine isolated verisimilitude caught from the Penetralium of mystery, from being incapable of remaining content with half-knowledge."

It is true that Coleridge is a striking example of a poet incapable of reconciling his reasoning sense with his poetic intuition. But Keats overlooks the fact that there were poets who were not content with half-knowledge and who yet wrote great poetry. His view of Shakespeare possessing "negative Capability" "so enormously" is unhistoric. Shakespeare did not "reach after fact and reason" very often, it is true, but then there is in his work a whole continent of vast assumptions, of accepted facts and agreed reasons, which were impossible to the early nineteenth-century poet without his taking up a conscious and reasoning attitude towards them. Keats's attitude is that the poet does not have to takes sides about religion, philosophy, the social order, any more than a flower takes sides. But Shakespeare lived in the time of our greatest national unity, when there was, for all intents and purposes, only one side about the problems which distract Wordsworth, Coleridge and Shelley. The flower did not have to draw attention to itself, because it was rooted in a very rich soil. The balance of Keats's own position seems partly to lie in the fact that he had not realized how much that soil of assumptions and things which it was unnecessary to reason about had shrunk. He happily derived his own poetry from an elixir of literary experiences. It is curious that amongst all his acute and profound critical reflections it never occurs to him that Shakespeare's own experience was not primarily of literature but of nature and life. The dilemma of Wordsworth, Southey, Coleridge and Shelley was that they wanted to draw their strength from life, and directly they wanted this they were involved in taking sides and having opinions.

# PREFACE

The Romantic Movement was a crucial phase in the historic development which has led to the increasing isolation of poetry from the main streams of contemporary life and thought into a stream which is specialized. The background of this crisis was the French Revolution which offered poets the vision of a whole community living creatively, imaginatively, poetically, using modern political organization and techniques to shape a society according to the best impulses of the heart of man. But the French Revolution produced (like the Russian Revolution and other revolutions in our time) an alien, brutal, intractable, inhuman mechanical fatality from which the poets shrank. It drove the Lake poets —those early revolutionists—into complete reaction, as the later Russian Revolution drove Russian poets who had welcomed it to suicide.

The French Revolution is implicit in the works of the Romantics, conspicuous either by its presence or by its absence. Its general effect was to drive poets into themselves and to give them that self-consciousness about the choice of their subject-matter which has been characteristic of English poetry ever since. They either avoid a contemporary subject-matter or their approach to it is oblique, obscure or violent. Romantic poetry has furious outbursts against contemporary politicians and important men, particularly against Pitt, Castlereagh and the Prince Regent. These are the expletives of men who feel that they are not going to be listened to when they speak from the bitterness of their hearts. How different from the assured, powerful, effective satire of Pope.

The poet's eye had lost the power to roll "in a fine frenzy" from heaven to earth and from earth to heaven. It had to turn inwards and create a new heaven and a new earth of the imagination. In abandoning the connection with the actuality and the outwardness of the external world and society, it also abandoned the structure of logical argument and of outer reality. The romantic poet was doomed endlessly to invent, to spin the web, to produce new treasures from his inward eye and to be "original." This world of invention cannot be measured step by step against the concrete, related processes of actuality. What it can do is to create an ideal world of the spirit and the personality providing the reader with a vision, a total impression, which he can then compare with the total impression made on him by his day-to-day life. Shelley is his most impressive when he compares in a line or a phrase the total experience of monotonous life—"O world, O life, O time"—with the sense of unattained ideal possibilities. He is least successful when he tries to discipline his visions into a close criticism of events or a reasoned exposition of theories. Although there is a relation between the ideal of passages of *The Triumph of Life* or of *Prometheus Unbound* with the real, the ideal experience and the real experience cannot be brought into contact with each other; but like the sun and the earth, they exercise an influence on each other. To dismiss Shelley as an "ineffectual angel" or an impossible idealist, is to miss the point as completely as to accept him as a realist. The relation between his vision and reality is a hidden, secret one which may change the heart but which cannot criticize the world.

The method of Blake is quite different from that of the Romantics. Blake, indeed, is only a Romantic in some minor poems and in the technical respect of being in revolt against eighteenth-century classicism. He comes very near in the prophetic poems to bridging the gulf between the isolated poetic sensibility of great significance and outward events of great historic significance which are the two horns of Shelley's dilemma. The problem is to relate an intractable, inhuman, impersonal,

# PREFACE

violent contemporary development of history to the personal, the human, the imaginative at their intensest and most vivid within the sensibility of the poet. Blake's method—for a method it was —was to translate contemporary events into an elaborate system of poetic symbols. Although these symbols are cloudy and cryptic, they symbolize things which are outside the poet's inner world; and for this reason when he succeeds, Blake really does transform the history of his own time into a majestic poetry which is not interior poetry. A few lines of *The French Revolution* have an air of being about outward objects and events which one never finds in Shelley's political poetry:

As in day of havock and routed battle, among thick shades of dis-
    content,
On the soul-skirting mountains of sorrow, cold waving the Nobles
    fold round the King;
Each stern visage look'd up as with strong bands of iron, each strong
    limb bound down as with marble,
In flames of red wrath burning, bound in astonishment a quarter of
    an hour.

Then the King glow'd: his Nobles fold round, like the sun of old
    time quench'd in clouds;
In their darkness the King stood; his heart flam'd, and uttered a
    with'ring heat, and these words burst forth:

"The nerves of five thousand years' ancestry tremble, shaking the
    heavens of France;
Throbs of anguish beat on brazon war foreheads, they descend and
    look into their graves.
I see thro' darkness, thro' clouds rolling round me, the spirits of
    ancient Kings
Shivering over their bleach'd bones; round them their counsellors look
    up from the dust,
Crying: 'Hide from the living! Our bonds and our prisoners shout in
    the open field,

'Hide in the nether earth! Hide in the bones! Sit obscured in the
    hollow scull!
'Our flesh is corrupted, and we wear away. We are not numbered
    among the living. Let us hide
'In stones, among roots of trees. The prisoners have burst their dens.
'Let us hide; let us hide in the dust; and plague and wrath and tempest
    shall cease.' "

He ceas'd, silent pondering; his brows folded heavy, his forehead was
    in affliction.
Like the central fire, from the window he saw his vast armies spread
    over the hills,
Breathing red fires from man to man, and from horse to horse: then
    his bosom
Expanded like starry heaven; he sat down: his nobles took their
    ancient seats.

Then the ancientest Peer, Duke of Burgundy, rose from the Mon-
    arch's right hand, red as wines
From his mountains; an odour of war, like a ripe vineyard, rose from
    his garments,
And the chamber became as a clouded sky; o'er the council he
    stretch'd his red limbs,
Cloth'd in flames of crimson. . . .

This writing has all the fantastic qualities of Blake's paintings,
an imaginative power certainly stronger than that of Shelley and
Keats. Yet the picture is concrete. We feel that Blake is writing
of a real king, real nobles and a real revolution. The magnificent
imagery is a robe which the events wear, but Blake never loses a
certain painstaking humility before the facts. He is setting out to
describe the French Revolution as he sees it from Lambeth. He
refers to the Louvre, to the Bastille, to Necker at Geneva and to
Mirabeau. A penetrating awe before things as they are glows
through his images until they almost lose their identity, but
it does not transform them into subjective phantoms. The passage

# PREFACE

I have quoted offers a solution to the romantic dilemma. The solution is a Biblical vision of the events amidst which we live which sees them in their relation to the greatest changes in past history. Blake has historic sense, if historic sense is, in part at least, to see the whole of the past struggles of humanity assumed into the lives and struggles of people now living. What he lacks, of course, is a familiarity with the details of the events he describes, amongst which he moves uneasily like a child of great genius in a world of stupefying giants. Yet there are moments in Blake's prophetic books when one has glimpses of a poetic vision which might have interpreted the poverty and the prosperity, the materialism and the aspirations of the nineteenth century as a passage in human events at once as base and as majestic as a chapter of Old Testament history.

The romantic poet is divorced from history, which he ends by despising. Instead of seeing into it, he sees through it onto "faery lands forlorn." This is not fair to Shelley whose fairies, witches and goddesses are charged with electricity to transform society. Yet the essence of romanticism is not revolution, but the search for a pure poetic experience. By this I mean something different from an experience which is poetic in the sense that it can best be expressed in poetry. The poetic experience of the Romantics is, rather, that kind of experience which in life gives sensation nearest to that which poetry gives in literature. Often this is an experience scarcely capable of being expressed in words. It lurks behind and beyond the words in Wordsworth's memories of his joy in nature when he was a child; in Keats's pursuit of sensation through poetry (the taste of a peach, the bite of a pearly neck, the sense of a mystery of poets before him); in Shelley's search for a woman who is the sister of his own spirit.

If the Romantics were realists in their aims, one would have to

regard several of them as decadents. Indeed, there are critics who
have conscientiously set down all the incest, perversion and
neurosis which occur in their poems, in order to reach that con-
clusion, whilst there are critics who have psychoanalyzed Words-
worth, Shelley and even Keats. But we need only mention the
works of Verlaine, Swinburne, Francis Thompson, Coventry
Patmore, Rossetti, for example, to become conscious of a dis-
tinction. In the poems of these later poets there are passages
which have a direct or covert reference to sexual appetite, usually
either of an ashamed or else of a too exhibitionist kind. In
Wordsworth, Byron, Shelley and Keats there is no such awkward
fleshliness. In Byron and Keats there are, indeed, passages of
sensuality; in Wordsworth there is an occasional sexual tender-
ness; in Shelley there is a passionate identification of spiritual
with physical union. The sexual motive is recognized and it is
organized into the spiritual vision of romantic poetry, so that
when we find examples of incest and perversion, we should think
twice before concluding that these are projections into their
poetry of vicious habits or vicious wishes. I do not mean that
there was no morbidity in Shelley: I do mean that one must not
conclude that what seems perverse in his poetry corresponds to
perverse traits in his character. I think that if there were such
correspondence, it would have an involuntary obsessive nature
which would be evident, as it is in the work of Swinburne. No.
Shelley's (and for that matter, Byron's) insistence of incest is
not either a projection of their physical wishes into their poetry
or propaganda for vice. It is a way of insisting that in their poetry
they were creating an ideal world where the rules of the real
world do not apply. It was an assertion of the superiority of the
spirit over the body, through their poetry where the union of
brother and sister spirits permits of the physical union of their

bodies. What Shelley is trying to teach is not a world of decadence but a world free from the dictates of morality and every reality. Thus the Romantics should be discussed not for morbidity and perversion which they are supposed to show in some of their poems but for their attitude towards morality. Romanticism is not a "decadent" movement. But from a moralist's point of view it may be an immoral one, because it seeks to imagine a world where there is no immorality in personal relations between human beings and where the only crimes are public ones. Ultimately, also, romanticism preaches a too easy liberation of the spirit from the body by the poetic. The faith of the Romantics (in Shelley, Byron and Keats) is that if the world centered on the romantic vision there would be no such thing as a human tragedy.

As I have said, there are morbid elements in these poets which it may amuse certain critics to pick out and classify. But as a whole their poetic vision cannot be labeled healthy or unhealthy, decadent or undecadent. Such terms are irrelevant because romanticism is in no way representational. Romanticism no more represents the "unconscious" than the "conscious," it is as far removed from surrealism as from realism or "social realism." Its aim is the creation of an ideal world through the active creating of the imagination. The peculiarity of this world is its impulsiveness, its waywardness, the extent to which it is personal to the poet himself and divorced from actuality, supernatural or human authority, and from any system of consistent thought.

This divorce of the imagination from the real gives Keats and Shelley an unreality which they can scarcely have wished. When their poetry seems most real, it produces what is only an illusion of reality. The way of testing the extent of this illusion is to

compare romantic poetry with other poetry on similar themes.
Here is Keats on Death, in a famous passage:

> Darkling I listen; and, for many a time
> I have been half in love with easeful Death,
> Call'd him soft names in many a mused rhyme,
> To take into the air my quiet breath;
> Now more than ever it seems rich to die,
> To cease upon the midnight with no pain. . . .

Here is John Donne on the same subject:

> Thou hast made me. And shall thy work decay?
> Repaire me now, for now my end doth haste,
> I runne to death, and death meets me as fast,
> And all my pleasures are like yesterday;
> I dare not move my dimme eyes any way,
> Despaire behind, and death before doth cast
> Such terrour, and my feeble flesh doth waste
> By sinne in it, which it t'wards hell doth weigh. . . .

The first passage is to dream about dying. The second is to
wake and to become conscious of what it is to die.

It is interesting to consider a phrase which might well occur
in a poem of Keats or Shelley, torn from its context, and then
considered restored to its context. Such a phrase is "Church-bells
beyond the stars heard." What does this suggest, if one thinks
of it as a fragment from a sonnet of Keats? It suggests, I think,
a picture of space, of the night, with glittering stars, and beyond
the stars a vast and shadowy tower filled with the sound of
bells which call across great distances. It is a phrase which calls
to mind the "huge cloudy symbols of a high romance" of the
sonnet beginning "When I have fears that I may cease to be,"
which ends with the words:

> on the shore
> *Of the wide world I stand alone, and think*
> *Till love and fame to nothingness do sink,*

A sonnet which confronts us with the thought that there is nothing outside the mighty symbols which can be traced by the imagination.

I quote now the whole poem by George Herbert from which I have taken one phrase. There is a point in quoting the whole of the poem since it provides a useful background against which to set the Romantics.—The poem is the famous Prayer, by George Herbert:

> *Prayer, the Church's banquet, Angel's age,*
> *God's breath in man returning to his birth,*
> *The soul in paraphrase, heart in pilgrimage,*
> *The Christian plummet sounding heaven and earth;*
>
> *Engine against the Almighty, sinner's tower,*
> *Reversed thunder, Christ-side-piercing spear,*
> *The six days' world-transposing in an hour,*
> *A kind of tune, which all things hear and fear;*
>
> *Softness, and peace, and joy, and love, and bliss,*
> *Exalted Manna, gladness of the best,*
> *Heaven in ordinary, man well drest,*
> *The milky way, the bird of Paradise,*
>
> *Church-bells beyond the stars heard, the soul's blood,*
> *The land of spices, something understood.*

Every line here can be measured against a scale of the values to which the poem refers. The precise and concrete mysteries of the Church press through the imagery of the poem, giving it a shape as architectural as a Church itself. When we come to our phrase "Church-bells beyond the stars heard," in a sense it shrinks and becomes less grandiose than it would be in a sonnet full of "cloudy symbols of a high romance." But what it loses in vague immensity it gains in sublime authority and crystal clarity.

The Romantics are, of course, seeking another experience. Theirs is the shaping spirit of the poet moving in emptiness over the universe and imagining that it is in contact with other shaping forces—Nature in Wordsworth, Beauty in Keats, Humanity in Shelley. A sense of emptiness, of separation from God and society, and of a search for a sensation which, though poetic, lies beyond poetry and is never completely expressed in words, is the romantic spirit. This spirit evaporates directly there is an awareness of the solid and external (as apart from the spiritual and interior) aspect of things, or a sense of being involved in the everyday processes of a human cause, or an aesthetic purpose realizable within the form which may itself, to all appearances, be romantic. Thus the Romantics themselves are romantics only intermittently. Keats in the late poems to Fanny Brawne is confronted by a reality which shuts him out of a world where fulfillment is to be found only in the imagination. Wordsworth finds himself during the Napoleonic wars fully in sympathy with the grandiloquent sentiments of the English conservative press. His poetry becomes invocative, magnificent, objective, with a real grasp of the ends and means of the struggle against Napoleon, combined with a critical awareness of the failings of the English system and temperament, and it is only very faintly stupid. Shelley and Coleridge freeze themselves out of the romantic mood with noble public sentiment. When Tennyson writes *Mariana*, the lyrics from the *Princess*, and many other poems in the romantic manner, the goal achieved by an aesthetic success prevents one looking beyond the poetry to the romantic experience. These poems are hard and perfect objects, jewels exquisitely carved, but their romanticism is only a manner and a means; the end has been abandoned with the solid opaque achievement of the form. Indeed, the Victorian age involved the poets too much in its materialism for the dissatisfaction and the isolation from society, which were the romantic impulse, to continue. Only in the peculiar circumstances of Emily Brontë does one get a sense of that isolation, that unreality, that secret inexpressible experience, which leads to the pure, desperate creation of beauty in a spacious emptiness of the Romantics.

## The Choice of These Poems

In choosing the poems for this anthology, I have had a few principles in mind, without feeling myself bound too strictly to them.

First and foremost, was to remember that this is a romantic anthology. It illustrates romanticism and the Romantic Movement more than it represents the work of poets. I have, therefore, chosen the romantic poems of these poets before choosing other ones. In the case of Tennyson, who wrote only a very few poems which I consider romantic, I have chosen very few poems.

Tennyson at one end and Blake at the other, I did not feel sufficiently involved in romanticism for me to be justified in selecting more than a few of their poems which give a taste of their relation to the movement. But when it comes to poet really involved, such as Byron, Coleridge, Keats and Shelley, I have felt that whilst showing them as Romantics, I should also show the less romantic Keats of the cruel Lines to Fanny and the coarse Keats of Tasting Eve's Apple, and so with the other poets; the reader will see that where I have had to make a wide selection of poems I have tried to indicate the lines along which a selection would be representative of every aspect of their poetry

Only with Shelley and Keats can it be said, though, that the present selection gives a fairly complete picture of their powers. I have concentrated largely on the romantic side of Coleridge; with Byron and with Wordsworth the anthologist is baffled: one cannot choose their worse poems, yet their best poems are nearly all very well-known already. The truth is that for the reader who wishes to have any grasp of Byron and Wordsworth, even more than with other poets, he must read a great many pages and wade through a great many untidinesses: he must read the whole of the *Prelude* and the *Excursion* of Wordsworth, and at least the first half or three-quarters of Byron's *Don Juan*.

Wordsworth's Sonnets include perhaps the least romantic poetry he wrote. But they do permit of some originality of choice, because, for some reason, only the most famous ones are usually anthologized: for this reason I have chosen what may seem a disproportionate number.

There are more pages by Shelley than by any other poet in the volume. This does not mean that I consider Shelley more important than Wordsworth or than Keats. It means simply that, if there was a possibility of making a representative selection of his poems, it was worth the cost of what may seem an effect of disproportion.

Some readers may be exacerbated at my choosing "bits" of long poems. But, firstly, when I have only chosen long fragments, they are always passages complete in themselves of poems impossible to print in full. Secondly, when I have chosen shorter but still large fragments from some of Shelley's longer poems, I have done so because I suspect that very few readers ("You! hypocrite lecteur!—mon semblable,—mon frère!) living are likely to proceed very far with such poems of The Revolt of Islam, which nevertheless contains some beautiful things worth calling

# PREFACE

attention to. When I have quoted very short passages—some-
times only of a line or so in length—I have done so for the critical
purpose of drawing attention to some beautiful fragment likely
to be lost in a stream.

Lastly, I have not been afraid to choose plums—even though
I have shied at some of them. I think that an anthology claiming
to be a *romantic* anthology should contain at least a fair selec-
tion of some of the greatest romantic poems: and some of these
happen to be very famous ones.

My hope is that this selection will provide readers with the
satisfaction of meeting old friends, combined with the greater
satisfaction of meeting new ones, combined with the still greater
satisfaction of being encouraged to go out to seek those still
newer ones who have only dropped a hint of their presence in
these pages.

The titles of the Fragments by Beddoes are those provided by
Mr. F. L. Lucas in his excellent selection, published by the
Cambridge Press.

S. Sp.

# WILLIAM BLAKE

*To the Evening Star*

Thou fair-haired angel of the Evening,
Now whilst the sun rests on the mountains, light
Thy bright torch of love—thy radiant crown
Put on, and smile upon our evening bed!
Smile on our loves; and while thou drawest the
Blue curtains of the sky, scatter thy silver dew
On every flower that shuts its sweet eyes
In timely sleep. Let thy West Wind sleep on
The lake; speak silence with thy glimmering eyes
And wash the dusk with silver.—Soon, full soon,
Dost thou withdraw; then the wolf rages wide,
And the lion glares through the dun forest:
The fleeces of our flocks are covered with
Thy sacred dew; protect them with thine influence!

# WILLIAM BLAKE

*Song*

How sweet I roam'd from field to field,
    And tasted all the summer's pride,
Till I the prince of love beheld,
    Who in the sunny beams did glide!

He shew'd me lilies for my hair,
    And blushing roses for my brow;
He led me through his gardens fair,
    Where all his golden pleasures grow.

With sweet May dews my wings were wet,
    And Phoebus fir'd my vocal rage;
He caught me in his silken net,
    And shut me in his golden cage.

He loves to sit and hear me sing,
    Then, laughing, sports and plays with me;
Then stretches out my golden wing,
    And mocks my loss of liberty.

*To the Muses*

Whether on Ida's shady brow,
   Or in the chambers of the East,
The chambers of the sun, that now
   From antient melody have ceas'd;

Whether in Heav'n ye wander fair,
   Or the green corners of the earth,
Or the blue regions of the air,
   Where the melodious winds have birth;

Whether on chrystal rocks ye rove,
   Beneath the bosom of the sea
Wand'ring in many a coral grove,
   Fair Nine, forsaking Poetry!

How have you left the antient love
   That bards of old enjoy'd in you!
The languid strings do scarcely move!
   The sound is forc'd, the notes are few!

# WILLIAM BLAKE

*The Sick Rose*

O Rose, thou art sick!
The invisible worm
That flies in the night,
In the howling storm,

Has found out thy bed
Of crimson joy,
And his dark secret love
Does thy life destroy.

*Never Seek to Tell Thy Love*

Never seek to tell thy love
Love that never told can be;
For the gentle wind does move
Silently, invisibly.

I told my love, I told my love,
I told her all my heart,
Trembling, cold, in ghastly fears—
Ah, she doth depart.

Soon as she was gone from me
A traveller came by
Silently, invisibly—
O, was no deny.

# WILLIAM BLAKE

*London*

I wander thro' each charter'd street,
Near where the charter'd Thames does flow,
And mark in every face I meet
Marks of weakness, marks of woe.

In every cry of every Man,
In every Infant's cry of fear,
In every voice, in every ban,
The mind-forg'd manacles I hear.

How the chimney-sweeper's cry
Every black'ning church appals;
And the hapless soldier's sigh
Runs in blood down palace walls.

But most thro' midnight streets I hear
How the youthful harlot's curse
Blasts the new-born infant's tear,
And blights with plagues the marriage hearse.

# WILLIAM BLAKE

*The Book of Thel*

## Thel's Motto

Does the Eagle know what is in the pit?
Or wilt thou go ask the Mole?
Can Wisdom be put in a silver rod?
Or Love in a golden bowl?

### I

The daughters of the Seraphim led round their sunny flocks,
All but the youngest: she in paleness sought the secret air,
To fade away like morning beauty from the mortal day:
Down by the river of Adona her soft voice is heard,
And thus her gentle lamentation falls like morning dew:

"O life of this our spring! why fades the lotus of the water,
"Why fade these children of the spring, born but to smile & fall?
"Ah! Thel is like a wat'ry bow, and like a parting cloud;
"Like a reflection in a glass; like shadows in the water;
"Like dreams of infants, like a smile upon an infant's face;
"Like the dove's voice; like transient day; like music in the air.
"Ah! gentle may I lay me down, and gentle rest my head,
"And gentle sleep the sleep of death, and gentle hear the voice
"Of him that walketh in the garden in the evening time."

# WILLIAM BLAKE

The Lilly of the valley, breathing in the humble grass,
Answer'd the lovely maid and said: "I am a wat'ry weed,
"And I am very small and love to dwell in lowly vales;
"So weak, the gilded butterfly scarce perches on my head.
"Yet I am visited from heaven, and he that smiles on all
"Walks in the valley and each morn over me spreads his hand,
"Saying, 'Rejoice, thou humble grass, thou new-born lilly flower,
" 'Thou gentle maid of silent valleys and of modest brooks;
" 'For thou shalt be clothed in light, and fed with morning
   manna,
" 'Till summer's heat melts thee beside the fountains and the
   springs
" 'To flourish in eternal vales.' Then why should Thel complain?
"Why should the mistress of the vales of Har utter a sigh?"

She ceas'd & smil'd in tears, then sat down in her silver shrine.

Thel answer'd: "O thou little virgin of the peaceful valley,
"Giving to those that cannot crave, the voiceless, the o'ertired;
"Thy breath does nourish the innocent lamb, he smells thy
   milky garments,
"He crops thy flowers while thou sittest smiling in his face,
"Wiping his mild and meekin mouth from all contagious taints.
"Thy wine doth purify the golden honey; thy perfume,
"Which thou dost scatter on every little blade of grass that
   springs,
"Revives the milked cow, & tames the fire-breathing steed.
"But Thel is like a faint cloud kindled at the rising sun:
"I vanish from my pearly throne, and who shall find my place?"

"Queen of the vales," the Lilly answer'd, "ask the tender cloud,
"And it shall tell why it glitters in the morning sky,
"And why it scatters its bright beauty thro' the humid air.
"Descend, O little Cloud, & hover before the eyes of Thel."
The Cloud descended, and the Lilly bow'd her modest head
And went to mind her numerous charge among the verdant grass.

## II

"O Little Cloud," the virgin said, "I charge thee tell to me
"Why thou complainest not when in one hour thou fade away:
"Then we shall seek thee, but not find. Ah! Thel is like to thee:
"I pass away: yet I complain, and no one hears my voice."

The Cloud then shew'd his golden head & his bright form
        emerg'd,
Hovering and glittering on the air before the face of Thel.

"O virgin, know'st thou not our steeds drink of the golden springs
"Where Luvah doth renew his horses? Look'st thou on my youth,
"And fearest thou, because I vanish and am seen no more,
"Nothing remains? O maid, I tell thee, when I pass away
"It is to tenfold life, to love, to peace and raptures holy:
"Unseen descending, weigh my light wings upon balmy flowers,
"And court the fair-eyed dew to take me to her shining tent:
"The weeping virgin, trembling kneels before the risen sun,
"Till we arise link'd in a golden band and never part,
"But walk united, bearing food to all our tender flowers."

WILLIAM BLAKE

"Dost thou, O little Cloud? I fear that I am not like thee,
"For I walk thro' the vales of Har, and smell the sweetest flowers,
"But I feed not the little flowers; I hear the warbling birds,
"But I feed not the warbling birds; they fly and seek their food:
"But Thel delights in these no more, because I fade away;
"And all shall say, 'Without a use this shining woman liv'd,
"'Or did she only live to be at death the food of worms?'"

The Cloud reclin'd upon his airy throne and answer'd thus:

"Then if thou art the food of worms, O virgin of the skies,
"How great thy use, how great thy blessing! Every thing that lives
"Lives not alone nor for itself. Fear not, and I will call
"The weak worm from its lowly bed, and thou shalt hear its voice.
"Come forth, worm of the silent valley, to thy pensive queen."

The helpless worm arose, and sat upon the Lilly's leaf,
And the bright Cloud sail'd on, to find his partner in the vale.

### III

Then Thel astonish'd view'd the Worm upon its dewy bed.

"Art thou a Worm Image of weakness, art thou but a Worm?
"I see thee like an infant wrapped in the Lilly's leaf.
"Ah! weep not, little voice, thou canst not speak, but thou canst
    weep.
"Is this a Worm? I see thee lay helpless & naked, weeping,
"And none to answer, none to cherish thee with mother's smiles."
   The Clod of Clay heard the Worm's voice & rais'd her pitying
    head:
She bow'd over the weeping infant, and her life exhal'd
In milky fondness: then on Thel she fix'd her humble eyes.

40]

"O beauty of the vales of Har! we live not for ourselves.
"Thou seest me the meanest thing, and so I am indeed.
"My bosom of itself is cold, and of itself is dark;
"But he, that loves the lowly, pours his oil upon my head,
"And kisses me, and binds his nuptial bands around my breast,
"And says: 'Thou mother of my children, I have loved thee
" 'And I have given thee a crown that none can take away.'
"But how this is, sweet maid, I know not, and I cannot know;
"I ponder, and I cannot ponder; yet I live and love."

The daughter of beauty wip'd her pitying tears with her white
    veil,
And said: "Alas! I knew not this, and therefore did I weep.
"That God would love a Worm I knew, and punish the evil foot
"That wilful bruis'd its helpless form; but that he cherish'd it
"With milk and oil I never knew, and therefore did I weep;
"And I complain'd in the mild air, because I fade away,
"And lay me down in thy cold bed, and leave my shining lot."

"Queen of the vales," the matron Clay answer'd, "I heard thy
    sighs,
"And all thy moans flew o'er my roof, but I have call'd them
    down.
"Wilt thou, O Queen, enter my house? 'Tis given thee to enter
"And to return: fear nothing, enter with thy virgin feet."

IV

The eternal gates' terrific porter lifted the northern bar:
Thel enter'd in & saw the secrets of the land unknown.
She saw the couches of the dead, & where the fibrous roots
Of every heart on earth infixes deep its restless twists:
A land of sorrow & of tears where never smile was seen.

# WILLIAM BLAKE

She wander'd in the land of clouds thro' valleys dark, list'ning
Dolours & lamentations; waiting oft beside a dewy grave
She stood in silence, list'ning to the voices of the ground,
Till to her own grave plot she came, & there she sat down,
And heard this voice of sorrow breathed from the hollow pit.

"Why cannot the Ear be closed to its own destruction?
"Or the glist'ning Eye to the poison of a smile?
"Why are Eyelids stor'd with arrows ready drawn,
"Where a thousand fighting men in ambush lie?
"Or an Eye of gifts & graces show'ring fruits & coined gold?
"Why a Tongue impress'd with honey from every wind?
"Why an Ear, a whirlpool fierce to draw creations in?
"Why a Nostril wide inhaling terror, trembling, & affright?
"Why a tender curb upon the youthful burning boy?
"Why a little curtain of flesh on the bed of our desire?"

The Virgin started from her seat, & with a shriek
Fled back unhinder'd till she came into the vales of Har.

# WILLIAM BLAKE

[From] *The French Revolution*

## Louis XVI

The noise of trampling, the wind of trumpets, smote the palace
    walls with a blast,
Pale and cold sat the King in midst of his peers, and his noble
    heart sunk, and his pulses
Suspended their motion; a darkness crept over his eyelids, and
    chill cold sweat
Sat round his brows faded in faint death; his peers pale, like
    mountains of the dead
Cover'd with dews of night, groaning, shaking forests and floods.
    The cold newt,
And snake, and damp toad on the kingly foot crawl, or croak on
    the awful knee,
Shedding their slime; in folds of the robe the crown'd adder
    builds and hisses
From stony brows; shaken the forests of France, sick the kings
    of nations,
And the bottoms of the world were open'd, and the graves of
    arch-angels unseal'd:
The enormous dead lift up their pale fires and look over the
    rocky cliffs.
A faint heat from their fires reviv'd the cold Louvre; the frozen
    blood reflow'd.

# WILLIAM BLAKE

Awful up rose the king; him the peers follow'd; they saw the
    courts of the Palace

Forsaken, and Paris without a soldier, silent; for the noise was
    gone up

And follow'd the army, and the Senate in peace sat beneath
    morning's beam.

*To H. C.*

Six Years Old

O thou! whose fancies from afar are brought;
Who of thy words dost make a mock apparel,
And fittest to unutterable thought
The breeze-like motion and the self-born carol;
Thou faery Voyager! that dost float
In such clear water, that thy Boat
May rather seem
To brood on air than on an earthly stream;
Suspended in a stream as clear as sky,
Where earth and heaven do make one imagery;
O blessed Vision! happy Child!
That art so exquisitely wild,
I think of thee with many fears
For what may be thy lot in future years.
   I thought of times when Pain might be thy guest,
Lord of thy house and hospitality;
And Grief, uneasy Lover! never rest
But when she sate within the touch of thee.
Oh! too industrious folly!
Oh! vain and causeless melancholy!
Nature will either end thee quite;
Or, lengthening out thy season of delight,

Preserve for thee, by individual right,
A young Lamb's heart among the full-grown flocks.
What hast Thou to do with sorrow,
Or the injuries of to-morrow?
Thou art a Dew-drop, which the morn brings forth,
Ill fitted to sustain unkindly shocks;
Or to be trail'd along the soiling earth;
A gem that glitters while it lives,
And no forewarning gives;
But, at the touch of wrong, without a strife
Slips in a moment out of life.

*Ruth*

When Ruth was left half desolate,
Her Father took another Mate;
And Ruth, not seven years old,
A slighted Child, at her own will
Went wandering over dale and hill,
In thoughtless freedom bold.

And she had made a Pipe of straw,
And from that oaten Pipe could draw
All sounds of winds and floods;
Had built a Bower upon the green,
As if she from her birth had been
An Infant of the woods.

Beneath her Father's roof, alone
She seemed to live; her thoughts her own;
Herself her own delight;
Pleased with herself, nor sad nor gay;
And passing thus the live-long day,
She grew to Woman's height.

There came a youth from Georgia's shore—
A military casque he wore,
With splendid feathers drest;
He brought them from the Cherokees;
The feathers nodded in the breeze,
And made a gallant crest.

# WILLIAM WORDSWORTH

From Indian blood you deem him sprung:
Ah no! he spake the English tongue,
And bore a Soldier's name;
And, when America was free
From battle and jeopardy,
He 'cross the ocean came.

With hues of genius on his cheek
In finest tones the youth could speak.
—While he was yet a Boy,
The moon, the glory of the sun,
And streams that murmur as they run,
Had been his dearest joy.

He was a lovely Youth! I guess
The panther in the wilderness
Was not so fair as he;
And, when he chose to sport and play,
No dolphin ever was so gay
Upon the tropic sea.

Among the Indians he had fought;
And with him many tales he brought
Of pleasure and of fear;
Such tales as told to any Maid
By such a Youth, in the green shade,
Were perilous to hear.

He told of Girls—a happy rout!
Who quit their fold with dance and shout,
Their pleasant Indian Town,
To gather strawberries all day long;
Returning with a choral song
When daylight is gone down.

He spake of plants divine and strange
That every hour their blossoms change,
Ten thousand lovely hues!
With budding, fading, faded flowers
They stand the wonder of the bowers
From morn to evening dews.

He told of the Magnolia, spread
High as a cloud, high over head!
The Cypress and her spire;
—Of flowers that with one scarlet gleam
Cover a hundred leagues, and seem
To set the hills on fire.

The Youth of green savannahs spake,
And many an endless, endless lake,
With all its fairy crowds
Of islands, that together lie
As quietly as spots of sky
Among the evening clouds.

And then he said, "How sweet it were
A fisher or a hunter there,
A gardener in the shade,
Still wandering with an easy mind
To build a household fire, and find
A home in every glade!

"What days and what sweet years! Ah me!
Our life were life indeed, with thee
So passed in quiet bliss,
And all the while," said he, "to know
That we were in a world of woe,
On such an earth as this!"

And then he sometimes interwove
Dear thoughts about a Father's love:
"For there," said he, "are spun
Around the heart such tender ties,
That our own children to our eyes
Are dearer than the sun.

"Sweet Ruth! and could you go with me
My helpmate in the woods to be,
Our shed at night to rear;
Or run my own adopted Bride,
A sylvan Huntress at my side,
And drive the flying deer!

"Beloved Ruth!"—No more he said.
The wakeful Ruth at midnight shed
A solitary tear:
She thought again—and did agree
With him to sail across the sea,
And drive the flying deer.

"And now, as fitting is and right,
We in the Church our faith will plight,
A Husband and a Wife."
Even so they did; and I may say
That to sweet Ruth that happy day
Was more than human life.

Through dream and vision did she sink,
Delighted all the while to think
That on those lonesome floods,
And green savannahs, she should share
His board with lawful joy, and bear
His name in the wild woods.

But as you have before been told,
This Stripling, sportive, gay, and bold,
And with his dancing crest
So beautiful, through savage lands
Had roamed about, with vagrant bands
Of Indians in the West.

The wind, the tempest roaring high,
The tumult of a tropic sky,
Might well be dangerous food
For him, a Youth to whom was given
So much of earth—so much of Heaven,
And such impetuous blood.

Whatever in those Climes he found
Irregular in sight or sound
Did to his mind impart
A kindred impulse, seemed allied
To his own powers, and justified
The workings of his heart.

Nor less, to feed voluptuous thought,
The beauteous forms of nature wrought,
Fair trees and lovely flowers;
The breezes their own languor lent;
The stars had feelings, which they sent
Into those gorgeous bowers.

Yet, in his worst pursuits, I ween
That sometimes there did intervene
Pure hopes of high intent:
For passions linked to forms so fair
And stately, needs must have their share
Of noble sentiment.

But ill he lived, much evil saw
With men to whom no better law
Nor better life was known;
Deliberately, and undeceived,
Those wild men's vices he received,
And gave them back his own.

His genius and his moral frame
Were thus impaired, and he became
The slave of low desires:
A Man who without self-control
Would seek what the degraded soul
Unworthily admires.

And yet he with no feigned delight
Had wooed the Maiden, day and night
Had loved her, night and morn:
What could he less than love a Maid
Whose heart with so much nature played?
So kind and so forlorn!

Sometimes, most earnestly, he said,
"O Ruth! I have been worse than dead;
False thoughts, thoughts bold and vain,
Encompassed me on every side
When first, in confidence and pride,
I crossed the Atlantic Main.

"It was a fresh and glorious world,
A banner bright that was unfurled
Before me suddenly:
I looked upon those hills and plains,
And seemed as if let loose from chains
To live at liberty.

"But wherefore speak of this? For now,
Sweet Ruth! with thee, I know not how,
I feel my spirit burn—
Even as the east when day comes forth;
And, to the west, and south, and north,
The morning doth return."

Full soon that purer mind was gone;
No hope, no wish remained, no one,—
They stirred him now no more;
New objects did new pleasure give,
And once again he wished to live
As lawless as before.

Meanwhile, as thus with him it fared,
They for the voyage were prepared,
And went to the sea-shore;
But, when they thither came, the Youth
Deserted his poor Bride, and Ruth
Could never find him more.

"God help thee, Ruth!"—Such pains she had,
That she in half a year was mad,
And in a prison housed;
And there she sang tumultuous songs,
By recollection of her wrongs,
To fearful passion rouzed.

Yet sometimes milder hours she knew,
Nor wanted sun, nor rain, nor dew,
Nor pastimes of the May,
—They all were with her in her cell;
And a wild brook with cheerful knell
Did o'er the pebbles play.

WILLIAM WORDSWORTH

When Ruth three seasons thus had lain,
There came a respite to her pain;
She from her prison fled;
But of the Vagrant none took thought;
And where it liked her best she sought
Her shelter and her bread.

Among the fields she breathed again:
The master-current of her brain
Ran permanent and free;
And, coming to the banks of Tone,
There did she rest; and dwell alone
Under the greenwood tree.

The engines of her pain, the tools
That shaped her sorrow, rocks and pools,
And airs that gently stir
The vernal leaves, she loved them still,
Nor ever taxed them with the ill
Which had been done to her.

A Barn her *winter* bed supplies;
But, till the warmth of summer skies
And summer days is gone,
(And all do in this tale agree)
She sleeps beneath the greenwood tree,
And other home hath none.

An innocent life, yet far astray!
And Ruth will, long before her day,
Be broken down and old:
Sore aches she needs must have! but less
Of mind, than body's wretchedness,
From damp, and rain, and cold.

54]

If she is pressed by want of food,
She from her dwelling in the wood
Repairs to a road-side;
And there she begs at one steep place,
Where up and down with easy pace
The horsemen-travellers ride.

That oaten Pipe of hers is mute,
Or thrown away; but with a flute
Her loneliness she cheers:
This flute, made of a hemlock stalk,
At evening in his homeward walk
The Quantock Woodman hears.

I, too, have passed her on the hills
Setting her little water-mills
By spouts and fountains wild—
Such small machinery as she turned
Ere she had wept, ere she had mourned,
A young and happy Child!

Farewell! and when thy days are told,
Ill-fated Ruth! in hallowed mould
Thy corpse shall buried be;
For thee a funeral bell shall ring,
And all the congregation sing
A Christian psalm for thee.

# WILLIAM WORDSWORTH

## *Resolution and Independence*

There was a roaring in the wind all night;
The rain came heavily and fell in floods;
But now the sun is rising calm and bright;
The birds are singing in the distant woods;
Over his own sweet voice the Stock-dove broods;
The Jay makes answer as the Magpie chatters;
And all the air is filled with pleasant noise of waters.

All things that love the sun are out of doors;
The sky rejoices in the morning's birth;
The grass is bright with rain-drops;—on the moors
The Hare is running races in her mirth;
And with her feet she from the plashy earth
Raises a mist; that, glittering in the sun,
Runs with her all the way, wherever she doth run.

I was a Traveller then upon the moor;
I saw the Hare that raced about with joy;
I heard the woods, and distant waters, roar;
Or heard them not, as happy as a Boy:
The pleasant season did my heart employ:
My old remembrances went from me wholly;
And all the ways of men, so vain and melancholy!

But, as it sometimes chanceth, from the might
Of joy in minds that can no farther go,
As high as we have mounted in delight
In our dejection do we sink as low,
To me that morning did it happen so;
And fears, and fancies, thick upon me came;
Dim sadness—and blind thoughts, I knew not, nor could
    name.

I heard the Sky-lark warbling in the sky;
And I bethought me of the playful Hare:
Even such a happy Child of earth am I;
Even as these blissful Creatures do I fare;
Far from the world I walk, and from all care;
But there may come another day to me—
Solitude, pain of heart, distress, and poverty.

My whole life I have lived in pleasant thought,
As if life's business were a summer mood;
As if all needful things would come unsought
To genial faith, still rich in genial good;
But how can He expect that others should
Build for him, sow for him, and at his call
Love him, who for himself will take no heed at all?

I thought of Chatterton, the marvellous Boy,
The sleepless Soul that perished in the pride;
Of Him who walked in glory and in joy
Following his plough, along the mountain-side:
By our own spirits are we deified:
We Poets in our youth begin in gladness;
But thereof comes in the end despondency and madness.

[57

Now, whether it were by peculiar grace,
A leading from above, a something given,
Yet it befell, that, in this lonely place,
When I with these untoward thoughts had striven,
Beside a Pool bare to the eye of Heaven
I saw a Man before me unawares:
The oldest Man he seemed that ever wore grey hairs.

As a huge Stone is sometimes seen to lie
Couched on the bold top of an eminence;
Wonder to all who do the same espy,
By what means it could thither come, and whence;
So that it seems a thing endued with sense:
Like a Sea-beast crawled forth, that on a shelf
Of rock or sand reposeth, there to sun itself;

Such seemed this Man, not all alive nor dead,
Nor all asleep—in his extreme old age:
His body was bent double, feet and head
Coming together in life's pilgrimage;
As if some dire constraint of pain, or rage
Of sickness felt by him in times long past,
A more than human weight upon his frame had cast.

Himself he propped, his body, limbs, and face,
Upon a long grey Staff of shaven wood:
And, still as I drew near with gentle pace,
Upon the margin of that moorish flood
Motionless as a Cloud the Old Man stood;
That heareth not the loud winds when they call;
And moveth all together, if it move at all.

At length, himself unsettling, he the Pond
Stirred with his Staff, and fixedly did look
Upon the muddy water, which he conned,
As if he had been reading in a book:
And now a stranger's privilege I took;
And, drawing to his side, to him did say,
"This morning gives us promise of a glorious day."

A gentle answer did the Old Man make,
In courteous speech which forth he slowly drew:
And him with further words I thus bespake,
"What occupation do you there pursue?
This is a lonesome place for one like you."
He answered, while a flash of mild surprise
Broke from the sable orbs of his yet-vivid eyes.

His words came feebly, from a feeble chest,
But each in solemn order followed each,
With something of a lofty utterance drest;
Choice word, and measured phrase; above the reach
Of ordinary men; a stately speech;
Such as grave Livers do in Scotland use,
Religious men, who give to God and Man their dues.

He told, that to these waters he had come
To gather Leeches, being old and poor:
Employment hazardous and wearisome!
And he had many hardships to endure:
From pond to pond he roamed, from moor to moor;
Housing, with God's good help, by choice or chance;
And in this way he gained an honest maintenance.

The Old Man still stood talking by my side;
But now his voice to me was like a stream
Scarce heard; nor word from word could I divide;
And the whole Body of the Man did seem
Like one whom I had met with in a dream;
Or like a man from some far region sent,
To give me human strength, by apt admonishment.


My former thoughts returned: the fear that kills;
And hope that is unwilling to be fed;
Cold, pain, and labour, and all fleshy ills;
And mighty Poets in their misery dead.
—Perplexed, and longing to be comforted,
My question eagerly did I renew,
"How is it that you live, and what is it you do?"


He with a smile did then his words repeat;
And said, that, gathering Leeches, far and wide
He travelled; stirring thus about his feet
The waters of the Pools where they abide.
"Once I could meet with them on every side;
But they have dwindled long by slow decay;
Yet still I persevere, and find them where I may."
While he was talking thus, the lonely place,
The Old Man's shape, and speech, all troubled me:
In my mind's eye I seemed to see him pace
About the weary moors continually,
Wandering about alone and silently.
While I these thoughts within myself pursued,
He, having made a pause, the same discourse renewed.

And soon with this he other matter blended,
Cheerfully uttered, with demeanour kind,
But stately in the main; and when he ended,
I could have laughed myself to scorn to find
In that decrepit Man so firm a mind.
"God," said I, "be my help and stay secure;
I'll think of the Leech-gatherer on the lonely moor!"

# WILLIAM WORDSWORTH

## The Solitary Reaper

Behold her, single in the field,
Yon solitary Highland Lass!
Reaping and singing by herself;
Stop here, or gently pass!
Alone she cuts, and binds the grain,
And sings a melancholy strain;
O listen! for the Vale profound
Is overflowing with the sound.

No Nightingale did ever chaunt
More welcome notes to weary bands
Of Travellers in some shady haunt,
Among Arabian Sands:
Such thrilling voice was never heard
In spring-time from the Cuckoo-bird,
Breaking the silence of the seas
Among the farthest Hebrides.

Will no one tell me what she sings?
Perhaps the plaintive numbers flow
For old, unhappy, far-off things,
And battles long ago:
Or is it some more humble lay,
Familiar matter of to-day?
Some natural sorrow, loss, or pain,
That has been, and may be again!

Whate'er the theme, the Maiden sang
As if her song could have no ending;
I saw her singing at her work,
And o'er the sickle bending;—
I listened—motionless and still;
And when I mounted up the hill,
The music in my heart I bore,
Long after it was heard no more.

# WILLIAM WORDSWORTH

*Elegiac Stanzas*

Suggested by a Picture of Peele Castle, in a Storm, Painted b
Sir George Beaumont

I was thy Neighbour once, thou rugged Pile!
Four summer weeks I dwelt in sight of thee:
I saw thee every day; and all the while
Thy Form was sleeping on a glassy sea.

So pure the sky, so quiet was the air!
So like, so very like, was day to day!
Whene'er I looked, thy Image still was there;
It trembled, but it never passed away.

How perfect was the calm! it seemed no sleep;
No mood, which season takes away, or brings:
I could have fancied that the mighty Deep
Was even the gentlest of all gentle Things.

Ah! then, if mine had been the Painter's hand,
To express what then I saw; and add the gleam,
The lustre, known to neither sea nor land,
But borrowed from the youthful Poet's dream;

I would have planted thee, thou hoary Pile!
Amid a world how different from this!
Beside a sea that could not cease to smile;
On tranquil land, beneath a sky of bliss.

A Picture had it been of lasting ease,
Elysian quiet, without toil and strife;
No motion but the moving tide, a breeze,
Or merely silent Nature's breathing life.

Such, in the fond illusion of my heart,
Such Picture would I at that time have made:
And seen the soul of truth in every part;
A faith, a trust, that could not be betrayed.

So once it would have been,—'tis so no more;
I have submitted to a new control:
A power is gone, which nothing can restore;
A deep distress hath humanized my Soul.

Not for a moment could I now behold
A smiling sea, and be what I have been:
The feeling of my loss will ne'er be old;
This, which I know, I speak with mind serene.

Then, Beaumont, Friend! who would have been the
    Friend,
If he had lived, of Him whom I deplore,
This Work of thine I blame not, but commend;
This sea in anger, and that dismal shore.

O 'tis a passionate work!—yet wise and well;
Well chosen is the spirit that is here;
That Hulk which labours in the deadly swell,
This rueful sky, this pageantry of fear!

And this huge Castle, standing here sublime,
I love to see the look with which it braves,
Cased in the unfeeling armour of old time,
The lightning, the fierce wind, and trampling waves.

Farewell, farewell the heart that lives alone,
Housed in a dream, at distance from the Kind!
Such happiness, wherever it be known,
Is to be pitied; for 'tis surely blind.

But welcome fortitude, and patient cheer,
And frequent sights of what is to be borne!
Such sights, or worse, as are before me here.—
Not without hope we suffer and we mourn.

# WILLIAM WORDSWORTH

## Lines Composed a Few Miles above Tintern Abbey, on Revisiting the Banks of the Wye During a Tour, July 13, 1798

Five years have past; five summers with the length
Of five long winters! and again I hear
These waters, rolling from their mountain-springs
With a soft inland murmur.—Once again
Do I behold these steep and lofty cliffs,
That on a wild secluded scene impress
Thoughts of more deep seclusion; and connect
The landscape with the quiet of the sky.
The day is come when I again repose
Here, under this dark sycamore, and view
These plots of cottage-ground, these orchard-tufts,
Which at this season, with their unripe fruits,
Are clad in one green hue, and lose themselves
'Mid groves and copses. Once again I see
These hedge-rows, hardly hedge-rows, little lines
Of sportive wood run wild: these pastoral farms,
Green to the very door; and wreaths of smoke
Sent up, in silence, from among the trees!
With some uncertain notice, as might seem
Of vagrant dwellers in the houseless woods,
Or of some Hermit's cave, where by his fire
The Hermit sits alone.
                              These beauteous forms,
Through a long absence, have not been to me

As is a landscape to a blind man's eye:
But oft, in lonely rooms, and 'mid the din
Of towns and cities, I have owed to them,
In hours of weariness, sensations sweet,
Felt in the blood, and felt along the heart;
And passing even into my purer mind,
With tranquil restoration:—feelings too
Of unremembered pleasure: such, perhaps,
As have no slight or trivial influence
On that best portion of a good man's life,
His little, nameless, unremembered acts
Of kindness and of love. Nor less, I trust,
To them I may have owed another gift,
Of aspect more sublime; that blessed mood,
In which the burthen of the mystery,
In which the heavy and the weary weight
Of all this unintelligible world,
Is lightened:—that serene and blessed mood,
In which the affections gently lead us on,—
Until, the breath of this corporeal frame
And even the motion of our human blood
Almost suspended, we are laid asleep
In body, and become a living soul:
While with an eye made quiet by the power
Of harmony, and the deep power of joy,
We see into the life of things.

                              If this
Be but a vain belief, yet, oh! how oft—
In darkness and amid the many shapes
Of joyless daylight; when the fretful stir
Unprofitable, and the fever of the world,

Have hung upon the beatings of my heart—
How oft, in spirit, have I turned to thee,
O sylvan Wye! thou wanderer thro' the woods,
How often has my spirit turned to thee!
And now, with gleams of half-extinguished thought,
With many recognitions dim and faint,
And somewhat of a sad perplexity,
The picture of the mind revives again:
While here I stand, not only with the sense
Of present pleasure, but with pleasing thoughts
That in this moment there is life and food
For future years. And so I dare to hope,
Though changed, no doubt, from what I was when first
I came along these hills; when like a roe
I bounded o'er the mountains, by the sides
Of the deep rivers, and the lonely streams,
Wherever nature led: more like a man
Flying from something that he dreads, than one
Who sought the thing he loved. For nature then
(The coarser pleasures of my boyish days,
And their glad animal movements all gone by)
To me was all in all.—I cannot paint
What then I was. The sounding cataract
Haunted me like a passion: the tall rock,
The mountain, and the deep and gloomy wood,
Their colours and their forms, were then to me
An appetite; a feeling and a love,
That had no need for a remoter charme,
By thought supplied, nor any interest
Unborrowed from the eye.—That time is past,
And all its aching joys are now no more,

[69

And all its dizzy raptures. Not for this
Faint I, nor mourn nor murmur; other gifts
Have followed; for such loss, I would believe,
Abundant recompense. For I have learned
To look on nature, not as in the hour
Of thoughtless youth; but hearing oftentimes
The still, sad music of humanity,
Nor harsh nor grating, though of ample power
To chasten and subdue. And I have felt
A presence that disturbs me with the joy
Of elevated thoughts; a sense sublime
Of something far more deeply interfused,
Whose dwelling is the light of setting suns,
And the round ocean and the living air,
And the blue sky, and in the mind of man:
A motion and a spirit, that impels
All thinking things, all objects of all thought,
And rolls through all things. Therefore am I still
A lover of the meadows and the woods,
And mountains; and of all that we behold
From this green earth; of all the mighty world
Of eye, and ear,—both what they half create,
And what perceive; well pleased to recognise
In nature and in language of the sense,
The anchor of my purest thoughts, the nurse,
The guide, the guardian of my heart, and soul
Of all my moral being.

                    Nor perchance,
If I were not this taught, should I the more
Suffer my genial spirits to decay:
For thou art with me here upon the banks

Of this fair river; thou my dearest Friend,
My dear dear Friend; and in the voice I catch
The language of my former heart, and read
My former pleasures in the shooting lights
Of thy wild eyes. Oh! yet a little while
May I behold in thee what I was once,
My dear dear Sister! and this prayer I make
Knowing that Nature never did betray
The heart that loved her; 'tis her privilege
Through all the years of this our life, to lead
From joy to joy: for she can so inform
The mind that is within us, so impress
With quietness and beauty, and so feed
With lofty thoughts, that neither evil tongues,
Rash judgements, nor the sneers of selfish men,
Nor greetings where no kindness is, nor all
The dreary intercourse of daily life,
Shall e'er prevail against us, or disturb
Our cheerful faith that all which we behold
Is full of blessings. Therefore let the moon
Shine on thee in thy solitary walk;
And let the misty mountain-winds be free
To blow against thee: and, in after years,
When these wild ecstasies shall be matured
Into a sober pleasure; when thy mind
Shall be a mansion for all lovely forms,
Thy memory be as a dwelling-place
For all sweet sounds and harmonies; oh! then,
If solitude, or fear, or pain, or grief,
Should be thy portion, with what healing thoughts
Of tender joy wilt thou remember me,

And these my exhortations! nor, perchance—
If I should be where I no more can hear
Thy voice, nor catch from thy wild eyes these gleams
Of past existence—wilt thou then forget
That on the banks of this delightful stream
We stood together; and that I, so long
A worshipper of Nature, hither came
Unwearied in that service: rather say
With warmer love—oh! with far deeper zeal
Of holier love. Nor wilt thou then forget,
That after many wanderings, many years
Of absence, these steep woods and lofty cliffs,
And this green pastoral landscape, were to me
More dear, both for themselves and for thy sake!

# WILLIAM WORDSWORTH

*There Was a Boy*

There was a Boy; ye know him well, ye cliffs
And islands of Winander!—many a time,
At evening, when the earliest stars began
To move along the edges of the hills,
Rising or setting, would he stand alone,
Beneath the trees, or by the glimmering lake;
And there, with fingers interwoven, both hands
Pressed closely palm to palm and to his mouth
Uplifted, he, as through an instrument,
Blew mimic hootings to the silent owls,
That they might answer him.—And they would shout
Across the watery vale, and shout again,
Responsive to his call,—with quivering peals,
And long halloos, and screams, and echoes loud
Redoubled and redoubled; concourse wild
Of jocund din! And, when there came a pause
Of silence such as baffled his best skill:
Then, sometimes, in that silence, while he hung
Listening, a gentle shock of mild surprise
Has carried far into his heart the voice
Of mountain-torrents; or the visible scene
Would enter unawares into his mind
With all its solemn imagery, its rocks,
Its woods, and that uncertain heaven received
Into the bosom of the steady lake.

This boy was taken from his mates, and died
In childhood, ere he was full twelve years old.
Pre-eminent in beauty is the vale
Where he was born and bred: the church-yard hangs
Upon a slope above the village-school;
And through that church-yard when my way has led
On summer-evenings, I believe, that there
A long half-hour together I have stood
Mute—looking at the grave in which he lies!

# WILLIAM WORDSWORTH

*The Prelude*

[*From*] Residence in France

    Among that band of Officers was one
Already hinted at, of other mold,
A Patriot, thence rejected by the rest
And with an oriental loathing spurn'd,
As of a different caste. A meeker man
Than this liv'd never, or a more benign
Meek, though enthusiastic. Injuries
Made him more gracious, and his nature then
Did breath its sweetness out most sensibly
As aromatic flowers on alpine turf
When foot hath crush'd them. He thro' the events
Of that great change wander'd in perfect faith,
As through a Book, an old Romance or Tale
Of Fairy, or some dream of actions wrought
Behind the summer clouds. By birth he rank'd
With the most noble, but unto the poor
Among mankind he was in service bound
As by some tie invisible, oaths profess'd
To a religious Order. Man he lov'd
As Man; and to the mean and the obscure
And all the homely in their homely works
Transferr'd a courtesy which had no air

Of condescension, but did rather seem
A passion and a gallantry, like that
Which he, a Soldier, in his idler day
Had pay'd to Woman; somewhat vain he was,
Or seem'd so, yet it was not vanity
But fondness, and a kind of radiant joy
That cover'd him about when he was bent
On works of love or freedom, or revolved
Complacently the progress of a cause,
Whereof he was a part; yet this was meek
And placid, and took nothing from the Man
That was delightful: oft in solitude
With him I did discourse about the end
Of civil government, and its wisest forms,
Of ancient prejudice, and chartered rights,
Allegiance, faith, and law by time matured,
Custom and habit, novelty and change,
Of self-respect, and virtue in the Few
For patrimonial honour set apart,
And ignorance in the labouring Multitude.
For he, an upright Man and tolerant,
Balanced these contemplations in his mind
And I, who at that time was scarcely dipp'd
Into the turmoil, had a sounder judgment
Than afterwards, carried about me yet
With less alloy to its integrity
The experience of past ages, as through help
Of Books and common life it finds its way
To youthful minds, by objects over near
Not press'd upon, nor dazzled or misled
By struggling with the crowd for present ends.

But though not deaf and obstinate to find
Error without apology on the side
Of those who were against us, more delight
We took, and let this freely be confess'd,
In painting to ourselves the miseries
Of royal Courts, and that voluptuous life
Unfeeling, where the Man who is of soul
The meanest thrives the most, where dignity,
True personal dignity, abideth not,
A light and cruel world, cut off from all
The natural inlets of just sentiment,
From lowly sympathy, and chastening truth,
Where good and evil never have that name,
That which they ought to have, but wrong prevails,
And vice at home. We added dearest themes,
Man and his noble nature, as it is
The gift of God and lies in his own power,
His blind desires and steady faculties
Capable of clear truth, the one to break
Bondage, the other to build Liberty
On firm foundations, making social life,
Through knowledge spreading and imperishable,
As just in regulation, and as pure
As individual in the wise and good.
We summon'd up the honorable deeds
Of ancient Story, thought of each bright spot
That could be found in all recorded time
Of truth preserv'd and error pass'd away,
Of single Spirits that catch the flame from Heaven,
And how the multitude of men will feed
And fan each other, thought of Sects, how keen

[77

They are to put the appropriate nature on,
Triumphant over every obstacle
Of custom, language, Country, love and hate,
And what they do and suffer for their creed,
How far they travel, and how long endure,
How quickly mighty Nations have been form'd
From least beginnings, how, together lock'd
By new opinions, scatter'd tribes have made
One body spreading wide as clouds in heaven.
To aspirations then of our own minds
Did we appeal; and finally beheld
A living confirmation of the whole
Before us in a People risen up
Fresh as the morning Star: elate we look'd
Upon their virtues, saw in rudest men
Self-sacrifice the firmest, generous love
And continence of mind, and sense of right
Uppermost in the midst of fiercest strife.

    Oh! sweet it is, in academic Groves,
Or such retirement, Friend! as we have known
Among the mountains, by our Rotha's Stream,
Greta or Derwent, or some nameless Rill,
To ruminate with interchange of talk
On rational liberty, and hope in Man,
Justice and peace; but far more sweet such toil,
Toil say I, for it leads to thoughts abstruse
If Nature then be standing on the brink
Of some great trial, and we hear the voice
Of one devoted, one whom circumstance
Hath call'd upon to embody his deep sense
In action, give it outwardly a shape,

And that of benediction to the world;
Then doubt is not, and truth is more than truth,
A hope it is and a desire, a creed
Of zeal by an authority divine
Sanction'd of danger, difficulty or death.
Such conversation under Attic shades
Did Dion hold with Plato, ripen'd thus
For a Deliverer's glorious task, and such,
He, on that ministry already bound,
Held with Eudemus and Timonides,
Surrounded by Adventurers in Arms,
When those two Vessels with their daring Freight
For the Sicilian Tyrant's overthrow
Sail'd from Zacynthus, philosophic war
Led by Philosophers. With harder fate,
Though like ambition, such was he, O Friend!
Of whom I speak, so Beaupuis (let the name
Stand near the worthiest of Antiquity)
Fashion'd his life, and many a long discourse
With like persuasion honor'd we maintain'd,
He on his part accoutred for the worst.
He perish'd fighting in supreme command
Upon the Border of the unhappy Loire
For Liberty against deluded Men,
His Fellow-countrymen, and yet most bless'd
In this, that he the fate of later times
Lived not to see, nor what we now behold
Who have as ardent hearts as he had then.

  Along that very Loire, with Festivals
Resounding at all hours, and innocent yet
Of civil slaughter was our frequent walk

Or in wide Forests of the neighbourhood,
High woods and over-arch'd, with open space
On every side, and footing many a mile,
In woven roots and moss smooth as the sea,
A solemn region. Often in such place
From earnest dialogues I slipp'd in thought
And let remembrance steal the other times
When Hermits from their sheds and caves forth stray'd
Walk'd by themselves, so met in shades like these,
And if a devious Traveller was heard
Approaching from a distance, as might chance,
With speed and echoes loud of trampling hoofs
From the hard floor reverberated, then
It was Angelica thundering through the woods
Upon the Palfrey, or that gentler Maid
Erminia, fugitive as fair as She.
Sometimes I saw, methought, a pair of Knights
Joust underneath the trees, that, as in storm,
Did rock above their heads; anon the din
Of boisterous merriment and music's roar,
With sudden Proclamation, burst from haunt
Of Satyrs in some viewless glade, with dance
Rejoicing o'er a Female in the midst,
A mortal Beauty, their unhappy Thrall;
The width of those huge Forests, unto me
A novel scene, did often in this way
Master my fancy, while I wander'd on
With that revered Companion. And sometimes
When to a Convent in a meadow green
By a brook-side we came, a roofless Pile,
And not by reverential touch of Time

Dismantled, but by violence abrupt,
In spite of those heart-bracing colloquies,
In spite of real fervour, and of that
Less genuine and wrought up within myself
I could not but bewail a wrong so harsh,
And for the matin Bell to sound no more
High on the topmost Pinnacle, a sign
Admonitory to the Traveller
First seen above the woods.
                          And when my Friend
Pointed upon occasion to the Site
Of Romorentin, home of ancient Kings,
To the imperial Edifice of Blois
Or to that rural Castle, name now slipp'd
From my remembrance, where a Lady lodg'd
By the first Francis wooed, and bound to him
In chains of mutual passion; from the Tower,
As a Tradition of the Country tells,
Practis'd to commune with the Royal Knight
By cressets and love-beacons, intercourse
'Twixt her high-seated Residence and his
Far off at Chambord on the Plain beneath:
Even here, though less than with the peaceful House
Religious, 'mid those frequent monuments
Of Kings, their vices and their better deeds,
Imagination, potent to enflame
At times with virtuous wrath and noble scorn,
Did also often mitigate the force
Of civic prejudice, the bigotry,
So call it, of a youthful Patriot's mind,
And on these spots with many gleams I look'd

Of chivalrous delight. Yet not the less,
Hatred of absolute rule, where will of One
Is law for all, and of that barren pride
In them who, by immunities unjust,
Betwixt the Sovereign and the People stand,
His helper and not theirs, laid stronger hold
Daily upon me, mix'd with pity too
And love; for where hope is there love will be
For the abject multitude. And when we chanc'd
One day to meet a hunger-bitten Girl,
Who crept along, fitting her languid gait
Unto a Heifer's motion, by a cord
Tied to her arm, and picking thus from the lane
Its sustenance, while the girl with her two hands
Was busy knitting, in a heartless mood
Of solitude, and at the sight my Friend
In agitation said, " 'Tis against *that*
Which we are fighting," I with him believed
Devoutly that a spirit was abroad
Which could not be withstood, that poverty
At least like this, would in a little time
Be found no more, that we should see the earth
Unswarthed in her wish to recompense
The industrious, and the lowly Child of Toil,
All institutes for ever blotted out
That legalised exclusion, empty pomp
Abolish'd, sensual state and cruel power
Whether by edict of the one or few,
And finally, as sum and crown of all,
Should see the People having a strong hand
In making their own Laws, whence better days

To all mankind. But, these things set apart,
Was not the single confidence enough
To animate the mind that ever turn'd
A thought to human welfare, that henceforth
Captivity by mandate without law
Should cease, and open accusation lead
To sentence in the hearing of the world
And open punishment, if not the air
Be free to breathe in, and the heart of Man
Dread nothing? Having touch'd this argument
I shall not, as my purpose was, take note
Of other matters which detain'd us oft
In thought or conversation, public acts,
And public persons, and the emotions wrought
Within our minds by the ever-varying wind
Of Record or Report which day by day
Swept over us; but I will here instead
Draw from obscurity a tragic Tale
Not in its spirit singular indeed
But haply worth memorial, as I heard
The events related by my patriot Friend
And others who had borne a part therein.


  Oh! happy time of youthful Lovers! thus
My Story may begin, Oh! balmy time
In which a Love-knot on a Lady's brow
Is fairer than the fairest Star in heaven!
To such inheritance of blessedness
Young Vaudracour was brought by years that had
A little overstepp'd his stripling prime.
A Town of small repute in the heart of France

[83

Was the Youth's Birth-place: there he vow'd his love
To Julia, a bright Maid, from Parents sprung
Not mean in their condition; but with rights
Unhonour'd of Nobility, and hence
The Father of the young Man, who had place
Among that order, spurn'd the very thought
Of such alliance. From their cradles up,
With but a step between their several homes
The pair had thriven together year by year
Friends, Playmates, Twins in pleasure, after strife
And petty quarrels had grown fond again,
Each other's advocate, each other's help,
Nor ever happy if they were apart:
A basis this for deep and solid love,
And endless constancy, and placid truth;
But what soever of such treasures might,
Beneath the outside of their youth, have lain
Reserv'd for mellower years, his present mind
Was under fascination; he beheld
A vision, and he lov'd the thing he saw.
Arabian Fiction never fill'd the world
With half the wonders that were wrought for him.
Earth liv'd in one great presence of the spring,
Life turn'd the meanest of her implements
Before his eyes to price above all gold,
The house she dwelt in was a sainted shrine,
Her chamber-window did surpass in glory
The portals of the East, all paradise
Could by the simple opening of a door
Let itself in upon him, pathways, walks,
Swarm'd with enchantment till his spirit sank

Beneath the burthen, overbless'd for life.
This state was theirs, till whether through effect
Of some delirious hour, or that the Youth,
Seeing so many bars betwixt himself
And the dear haven where he wish'd to be
In honourable wedlock with his love
Without a certain knowledge of his own,
Was inwardly prepared to turn aside
From law and custom, and entrust himself
To Nature for a happy end of all;
And thus abated of that pure reserve
Congenial to his loyal heart, with which
It would have pleas'd him to attend the steps
Of Maiden so divinely beautiful
I know not, but reluctantly must add
That Julia, yet without the name of Wife
Carried about her for a secret grief
The promise of a Mother.
                    To conceal
The threaten'd shame the Parents of the Maid
Found means to hurry her away by night
And unforewarn'd, that in a distant Town
She might remain shrouded in privacy,
Until the Babe was born. When morning came
The Lover thus bereft, stung with his loss
And all uncertain whither he should turn
Chafed like a wild beast in the toils; at length,
Following as his suspicions led, he found
O joy! sure traces of the fugitives,
Pursu'd them to the Town where they had stopp'd,
And lastly to the very House itself

Which had been chosen for the Maid's retreat.
The sequel may be easily divined,
Walks backwards, forwards, morning, noon and **night**
When decency and caution would allow
And Julia, who, whenever to herself
She happen'd to be left a moment's space,
Was busy at her casement, as a Swallow
About its nest, ere long did thus espy
Her Lover, thence a stolen interview
By night accomplish'd, with a ladder's help.

I pass the raptures of the Pair; such theme
Hath by a hundred Poets been set forth
In more delightful verse than skill of mine
Could fashion, chiefly by that darling Bard
Who told of Juliet and her Romeo,
And of the Lark's note heard before its time,
And of the streaks that lac'd the severing clouds
In the unrelenting East. 'Tis mine to tread
The humbler province of plain history,
And, without choice of circumstance, submissively
Relate what I have heard. The Lovers came
To this resolve, with which they parted, pleas'd
And confident, that Vaudracour should hie
Back to his Father's house, and there employ
Means aptest to obtain a sum of gold,
A final portion, even, if that might be,
Which done, together then take flight
To some remote and solitary place
Where they might live with no one to behold
Their happiness, or to disturb their love.
Immediately, and with this mission charg'd

Home to his Father's House the Youth return'd
And there remain'd a while without hint given
Of his design; but if a word were dropp'd
Touching the matter of his passion, still
In hearing of his Father, Vaudracour
Persisted openly that nothing less
Than death should make him yield up hope to be
A blessed Husband of the Maid he loved.

Incensed at such obduracy and slight
Of exhortations and remonstrances
The Father threw out threats that by a mandate
Bearing the private signet of the State
He should be baffled of his mad intent,
And that should cure him. From this time the Youth
Conceiv'd a terror, and by night or day
Stirr'd nowhere without Arms. Soon afterwards
His Parents to their Country Seat withdrew
Upon some feign'd occasion; and the Son
Was left with one Attendant in the house.
Retiring for his chamber for the night,
While he was entering at the door, attempts
Were made to seize him by three armed Men,
The instruments of ruffian power; the Youth
In the first impulse of his rage, laid one
Dead at his feet, and to the second gave
A perilous wound, which done, at sight
Of the dead Man, he peacefully resign'd
His Person to the Law, was lodged in prison,
And wore the fetters of a Criminal.

Through three weeks' space, by means which love devis'd
The Maid in her seclusion had received

Tidings of Vaudracour, and how he sped
Upon his enterprize. Thereafter came
A silence, half a circle did the moon
Complete, and then a whole, and still the same
Silence; a thousand thousand fears and hopes
Stirr'd in her mind; thoughts waking, thoughts of sleep
Entangled in each other, and at last
Self-slaughter seem'd her only resting-place.
So did she fear in her uncertainty.

At length, by interference of a Friend,
One who had sway at Court, the Youth regain'd
His liberty, on promise to sit down
Quietly in his Father's House, nor take
One step to reunite himself with her
Of whom his Parents disapproved: hard law
To which he gave consent only because
His freedom else could nowise be procured.
Back to his Father's house he went, remain'd
Eight days, and then his resolution fail'd:
He fled to Julia, and the words with which
He greeted her were these. "All right is gone,
Gone from me. Thou no longer now art mine,
I thine; a Murderer, Julia, cannot love
An innocent Woman; I behold thy face
I see thee and my misery is complete."
She could not give him answer; afterwards
She coupled with his Father's name some words
Of vehement indignation; but the Youth
Check'd her, nor would he hear of this; for thought
Unfilial, or unkind, had never once
Found harbour in his breast. The Lovers thus

United once again together lived
For a few days, which were to Vaudracour
Days of dejection, sorrow and remorse
For that ill deed of violence which his hand
Had hastily committed: for the Youth
Was of a loyal spirit, a conscience nice
And over tender for the trial which
His fate had call'd him to. The Father's mind,
Meanwhile, remain'd unchanged, and Vaudracour
Learn'd that a mandate had been newly issued
To arrest him on the spot. Oh pain it was
To part! he could not—and he linger'd still
To the last moment of his time, and then,
At dead of night with snow upon the ground,
He left the City, and in Villages
The most sequester'd of the neighbourhood
Lay hidden for the space of several days
Until the horseman bringing back report
That he was nowhere to be found, the search
Was ended. Back return'd the ill-fated Youth,
And from the House where Julia lodg'd (to which
He now found open ingress, having gain'd
The affection of the family, who lov'd him
Both for his own, and for the Maiden's sake)
One night retiring, he was seiz'd.—But here
A portion of the Tale may well be left
In silence, though my memory could add
Much how the Youth, and in short space of time,
Was travers'd from without, much, too, of thoughts
By which he was employ'd in solitude
Under privation and restraint, and what
Through dark and shapeless fear of things to come,

And what through strong compunction for the past
He suffer'd breaking down in heart and mind.
Such grace, if grace it were, had been vouchsafed
Or such effect had through the Father's want
Of power, or through his negligence ensued
That Vaudracour was suffer'd to remain,
Though under guard and without liberty,
In the same City with the unhappy Maid
From whom he was divided. So they fared
Objects of general concern, till, moved
With pity for their wrongs, the Magistrate,
The same who had plac'd the Youth in custody,
By application to the Minister
Obtain'd his liberty upon condition
That to his Father's house he should return.

He left his prison almost on the eve
Of Julia's travail; she had likewise been
As from the time indeed, when she had first
Been brought for secresy to this abode,
Though treated with consoling tenderness,
Herself a Prisoner, a dejected one,
Fill'd with a Lover's and a Woman's fears,
And whensoe'er the Mistress of the House
Enter'd the Room for the last time at night
And Julia with a low and plaintive voice
Said "You are coming then to lock me up"
The Housewife when these words, always the same,
Were by her Captive languidly pronounced
Could never hear them utter'd without tears.

A day or two before the Child-bed time
Was Vaudracour restored to her, and soon

As he might be permitted to return
Into her Chamber after the Child's birth
The Master of the Family begg'd that all
The household might be summon'd, doubting not
But that they might receive impressions then
Friendly to human kindness. Vaudracour
(This heard I from one present at the time)
Held up the new-born Infant in his arms
And kiss'd, and bless'd, and cover'd it with tears,
Uttering a prayer that he might never be
As wretched as his Father; then he gave
The Child to her who bare it, and she too
Repeated the same prayer, took it again
And muttering something faintly afterwards
He gave the Infant to the Standers-by,
And wept in silence upon Julia's neck.

Two months did he continue in the House,
And often yielded up himself to plans
Of future happiness. "You shall return,
Julia," said he, "and to your Father's House
Go with your Child, you have been wretched, yet
It is a town where both of us were born,
None will reproach you, for our loves are known,
With ornaments the prettiest you shall dress
Your Boy, as soon as he can run about,
And when he thus is at his play my Father
Will see him from the window, and the Child
Will by his beauty move his Grandsire's heart,
So that it shall be soften'd and our loves
End happily as they began." These gleams
Appear'd but seldom; oftener was he seen

Propping a pale and melancholy face
Upon the Mother's bosom, resting thus
His head upon one breast, while from the other
The Babe was drawing in its quiet food.
At other times, when he, in silence, long
And fixedly had look'd upon her face,
He would exclaim, "Julia, how much thine eyes
Have cost me!" During day-time when the Child
Lay in his cradle, by its side he sate,
Not quitting it an instant. The whole Town
In his unmerited misfortunes now
Took part, and if he either at the door
Or window for a moment with his Child
Appear'd, immediately the Street was throng'd
While others frequently without reserve
Pass'd and repass'd before the house to steal
A look at him. Oft at this time he wrote
Requesting, since he knew that the consent
Of Julia's Parents never could be gain'd
To a clandestine marriage, that his Father
Would from the birthright of an eldest Son
Exclude him, giving but, when it was done,
A sanction to his nuptials: vain request,
To which no answer was return'd. And now
From her own home the Mother of his Love
Arrived to apprise the Daughter of her fix'd
And last resolve, that, since all hope to move
The old Man's heart prov'd vain, she must retire
Into a Convent, and be there immured.
Julia was thunderstricken by these words,
And she insisted on a Mother's rights

WILLIAM WORDSWORTH

To take her Child along with her, a grant
Impossible, as she at last perceived;
The Persons of the house no sooner heard
Of this decision upon Julia's fate
Than everyone was overwhelm'd with grief
Nor could they frame a manner soft enough
To impart the tidings to the Youth; but great
Was their astonishment when they beheld him
Receive the news in calm despondency,
Composed and silent, without outward sign
Of even the least emotion; seeing this
When Julia scatter'd some upbraiding words
Upon his slackness he thereto return'd
No answer, only took the Mother's hand
Who lov'd him scarcely less than her own Child,
And kissed it, without seeming to be press'd
By any pain that 'twas the hand of one
Whose errand was to part him from his Love
For ever. In the city he remain'd
A season after Julia had retired
And in the Convent taken up her home
To the end that he might place his Infant Babe
With a fit nurse, which done, beneath the roof
Where now his little One was lodg'd he pass'd
The day entire, and scarcely could at length
Tear himself from the cradle to return
Home to his Father's House, in which he dwelt
Awhile, and then came back that he might see
Whether the Babe had gain'd sufficient strength
To bear removal. He quitted the same Town
For the last time, attendant by the side

[93

Of a close chair, a Litter or Sedan,
In which the Child was carried. To a hill
Which rose at a League's distance from the Town,
The Family of the house where he had lodged
Attended him, and parted from him there,
Watching below till he had disappeared
On the hill top. His eyes he scarcely took,
Through all that journey, from the Chair in which
The Babe was carried; and at every Inn
Or place at which they halted or reposed
Laid him upon his knees, nor would permit
The hands of any but himself to dress
The Infant or undress. By one of those
Who bore the Chair these facts, at his return,
Were told, and in relating them he wept.

   This was the manner in which Vaudracour
Departed with his Infant; and thus reach'd
His Father's House, where to the innocent Child
Admittance was denied. The young Man spake
No word of indignation or reproof,
But of his Father begg'd, a last request,
That a retreat might be assigned to him,
A house where in the Country he might dwell
With such allowance as his wants required
And the more lonely that the Mansion was
'Twould be more welcome. To a lodge that stood
Deep in a Forest, with leave given, at the age
Of four and twenty summers he retir'd;
And thither took with him his Infant Babe,
And one Domestic for their common needs,
An aged woman. It consoled him here
To attend upon the Orphan and perform

The office of a Nurse to his young Child
Which after a short time by some mistake
Or indiscretion of the Father, died.
The Tale I follow to its last recess
Of suffering or of peace, I know not which;
Theirs be the blame who caused the woe, not mine.

  From that time forth he never utter'd word
To any living. An Inhabitant
Of that same Town in which the Pair had left
So lively a remembrance of their griefs
By chance of business coming within reach
Of his retirement to the spot repair'd
With the intent to visit him: he reach'd
The house and only found the Matron there,
Who told him that his pains were thrown away,
For that her Master never uttered word
To living soul—not even to her. Behold
While they were speaking, Vaudracour approach'd;
But, seeing some one there, just as his hand
Was stretch'd towards the garden-gate, he shrunk,
And like a shadow glided out of view.
Shock'd at his savage outside, from the place
The visitor retired.
             Thus liv'd the Youth
Cut off from all intelligence with Man,
And shunning even the light of common day;
Nor could the voice of Freedom, which through France
Soon afterwards resounded, public hope,
Or personal memory of his own deep wrongs,
Rouse him: but in those solitary shades
His days he wasted, an imbecile mind.

# WILLIAM WORDSWORTH

*Ode*

Intimations of Immortality from
Recollections of early Childhood

> The Child is father of the Man;
> And I could wish my days to be
> Bound each to each by natural piety.

### 1

There was a time when meadow, grove, and stream,
The earth, and every common sight,
To me did seem
Apparelled in celestial light,
The glory and the freshness of a dream.
It is not now as it hath been of yore;—
Turn wheresoe'er I may,
By night or day,
The things which I have seen I now can see no more.

### 2

The Rainbow comes and goes,
And lovely is the Rose,
The Moon doth with delight
Look round her when the heavens are bare,
Waters on a starry night
Are beautiful and fair;

The sunshine is a glorious birth;
But yet I know, where'er I go,
That there hath past away a glory from the earth.

### 3

Now, while the birds thus sing a joyous song,
And while the young lambs bound
As to the tabor's sound,
To me alone there came a thought of grief:
A timely utterance gave that thought relief,
And I again am strong:
The cataracts blow their trumpets from the steep;
No more shall grief of mine the season wrong;
I hear the Echoes through the mountains throng,
The Winds came to me from the fields of sleep,
And all the earth is gay;
Land and Sea
Give themselves up to jollity,
And with the heart of May
Doth every Beast keep holiday;—
Thou Child of Joy,
Shout round me, let me hear thy shouts, thou happy
Shepherd-boy!

### 4

Ye blessed Creatures, I have heard the call
Ye to each other make; I see
The heavens laugh with you in your jubilee;
My heart is at your festival,
My head hath its coronal,
The fulness of your bliss, I feel—I feel it all.

Oh evil day! If I were sullen
While Earth herself is adorning,
    This sweet May-morning,
And the Children are culling
    On every side,
In a thousand valleys far and wide,
    Fresh flowers; while the sun shines warm,
And the Babe leaps up on his Mother's arm:—
    I hear, I hear, with joy I hear!
    —But there's a Tree, of many, one,
A single Field which I have looked upon,
Both of them speak of something that is gone:
        The Pansy at my feet
        Doth the same tale repeat:
Whither is fled the visionary gleam?
Where is it now, the glory and the dream?

### 5

Our birth is but a sleep and a forgetting:
The Soul that rises with us, our life's Star,
    Hath had elsewhere its setting,
    And cometh from afar:
    Not in entire forgetfulness,
    And not in utter nakedness,
But trailing clouds of glory do we come
    From God, who is our home:
Heaven lies about us in our infancy!
Shades of the prison-house begin to close
    Upon the growing Boy,
But He beholds the light, and whence it flows
    He sees it in his joy;

The Youth, who daily farther from the east
    Must travel, still is Nature's Priest,
    And by the vision splendid
    Is on his way attended;
At length the Man perceives it die away,
And fade into the light of common day.

### 6

Earth fills her lap with pleasures of her own;
Yearnings she hath in her own natural kind,
And even with something of a Mother's mind,
    And no unworthy aim,
    The homely Nurse doth all she can
To make her Foster-child, her Inmate Man,
    Forget the glories he hath known,
And that imperial palace whence he came.

### 7

Behold the Child among his new-born blisses,
A six years' Darling of a pigmy size!
See, where 'mid work of his own hand he lies,
Fretted by sallies of his mother's kisses,
With light upon him from his father's eyes!
See, at his feet, some little plan or chart,
Some fragment from his dream of human life,
Shaped by himself with newly-learned art;
    A wedding or a festival,
    A mourning or a funeral;
      And this hath now his heart,
    And unto this he frames his song:
      Then will he fit his tongue

To dialogues of business, love, or strife:
    But it will not be long
    Ere this be thrown aside,
    And with new joy and pride
The little Actor cons another part;
Filling from time to time his 'humorous stage'
With all the Persons, down to palsied Age,
That life brings with her in her equipage;
    As if his whole vocation
    Were endless imitation.

8

Thou, whose exterior semblance doth belie
    Thy Soul's immensity;
Thou best Philosopher, who yet dost keep
Thy heritage, thou Eye among the blind,
That, deaf and silent, read'st the eternal deep,
Haunted for ever by the eternal mind,—
    Mighty Prophet! Seer blest!
    On whom those truths do rest,
Which we are toiling all our lives to find,
In darkness lost, the darkness of the grave;
Thou, over whom thy Immortality
Broods like the Day, a Master o'er a slave,
A Presence which is not to be put by;
Thou little Child, yet glorious in the might
Of heaven-born freedom on thy being's height,
Why with such earnest pains dost thou provoke
The years to bring the inevitable yoke,
Thus blindly with thy blessedness at strife?

Full soon thy Soul shall have her earthly freight,
And custom lie upon thee with a weight,
Heavy as frost, and deep almost as life!

9

O joy! that in our embers
Is something that doth live,
That nature yet remembers
What was so fugitive!
The thought of our past years in me doth breed
Perpetual benediction: not indeed
For that which is most worthy to be blest;
Delight and liberty, the simple creed
Of Childhood, whether busy or at rest,
With new-fledged hope still fluttering in his breast:—
Not for these I raise
The song of thanks and praise;
But for those obstinate questionings
Of sense and outward things,
Fallings from us, vanishings;
Blank misgivings of a Creature
Moving about in worlds not realised,
High instincts before which our mortal Nature
Did tremble like a guilty thing surprised:
But for those first affections,
Those shadowy recollections,
Which, be they what they may,
Are yet the fountain light of all our day,
Are yet a master light of all our seeing;
Uphold us, cherish, and have power to make
Our noisy years seem moments in the being

Of the eternal Silence: truths that wake,
    To perish never;
Which neither listlessness, nor mad endeavour,
    Nor Man nor Boy,
Nor all that is at enmity with joy,
Can utterly abolish or destroy!
    Hence in a season of calm weather
    Though inland far we be,
Our Souls have sight of that immortal sea
    Which brought us hither,
    Can in a moment travel thither,
And see the Children sport upon the shore,
And hear the mighty waters rolling evermore.

10

Then sing, ye Birds, sing, sing a joyous song!
    And let the young Lambs bound
    As to the tabor's sound!
We in thought will join your throng,
    Ye that pipe and ye that play,
    Ye that through your hearts to-day
    Feel the gladness of the May!
What though the radiance which was once so bright
Be now for ever taken from my sight,
    Though nothing can bring back the hour
Of splendour in the grass, of glory in the flower;
    We will grieve not, rather find
    Strength in what remains behind;
    In the primal sympathy
    Which having been must ever be;

In the soothing thoughts that spring
Out of human suffering;
In the faith that looks through death,
In years that bring the philosophic mind.

11

And O, ye Fountains, Meadows, Hills and Groves,
Forebode not any severing of our loves!
Yet in my heart of hearts I feel your might;
I only have relinquished one delight
To live beneath your more habitual sway.
I love the Brooks, which down their channels fret,
Even more than when I tripped lightly as they:
The innocent brightness of a new-born Day
        Is lovely yet;
The Clouds that gather round the setting sun
Do take a sober colouring from an eye
That hath kept watch o'er man's mortality;
Another race hath been, and other palms are won.
Thanks to the human heart by which we live,
Thanks to its tenderness, its joys, and fears,
To me the meanest flower that blows can give
Thoughts that do often lie too deep for tears.

# WILLIAM WORDSWORTH

*Sonnet: September 1, 1802*

Driven from the soil of France, a Female came
From Calais with us, brilliant in array,—
A Negro Woman, like a Lady gay,
Yet downcast as a Woman fearing blame;
Meek, destitute, as seemed, of hope or aim
She sate, from notice turning not away,
But on all proffered intercourse did lay
A weight of languid speech,—or at the same
Was silent, motionless in eyes and face.
Meanwhile those eyes retained their tropic fire,
Which, burning independent of the mind,
Joined with the lustre of her rich attire
To mock the outcast—O ye Heavens, be kind!
And feel, thou Earth, for this afflicted Race!

# WILLIAM WORDSWORTH

*Sonnet: September, 1802*

Inland, within a hollow Vale, I stood;
And saw, while sea was calm and air was clear,
The Coast of France, the Coast of France how near!
Drawn almost into frightful neighbourhood.
I shrunk, for verily the barrier flood
Was like a Lake, or River bright and fair,
A span of waters; yet what power is there!
What mightiness for evil and for good!
Even so doth God protect us if we be
Virtuous and wise. Winds blow, and Waters roll,
Strength to the brave, and Power, and Deity,
Yet in themselves are nothing! One decree
Spake laws to them, and said that by the Soul
Only the Nations shall be great and free.

# WILLIAM WORDSWORTH

*Sonnet: Thought of a Briton on the Subjugation of Switzer-
land*

Two voices are there; one is of the Sea,
One of the Mountains; each a mighty Voice:
In both from age to age Thou didst rejoice,
They were thy chosen Music, Liberty!
There came a Tyrant, and with holy glee
Thou fought'st against Him; but hast vainly striven.
Thou from thy Alpine Holds at length art driven,
Where not a torrent murmurs heard by thee.
Of one deep bliss thine ear hath been bereft:
Then cleave, O cleave to that which still is left;
For, high-souled Maid, what sorrow would it be
That mountain Floods should thunder as before,
And Ocean bellow from his rocky shore,
And neither awful Voice be heard by thee!

# WILLIAM WORDSWORTH

*Sonnet: Written in London, September, 1802*

O Friend! I know not which way I must look
For comfort, being, as I am, opprest,
To think that now our Life is only drest
For show; mean handy-work of craftsman, cook,
Or groom!—We must run glittering like a Brook
In the open sunshine, or we are unblest:
The wealthiest man among us is the best:
No grandeur now in nature or in book
Delights us. Rapine, avarice, expense,
This is idolatry; and these we adore:
Plain living and high thinking are no more:
The homely beauty of the good old cause
Is gone; our peace, our fearful innocence,
And pure religion breathing household laws.

# WILLIAM WORDSWORTH

*Sonnet: There Is a Bondage Worse*

There is a bondage worse, far worse, to bear
Than his who breathes, by roof, and floor, and wall,
Pent in, a Tyrant's solitary Thrall:
'Tis his who walks about in the open air,
One of a Nation who, henceforth, must wear
Their fetters in their Souls. For who could be,
Who, even the best, in such condition, free
From self-reproach, reproach which he must share
With Human Nature? Never be it ours
To see the sun how brightly it will shine,
And know that noble Feelings, many Powers,
Instead of gathering strength, must droop and pine,
And earth with all her pleasant fruits and flowers
Fade, and participate in Man's decline.

# WILLIAM WORDSWORTH

## Sonnet: Composed by the Side of Grasmere Lake

Clouds, lingering yet, extend in solid bars
Through the grey west; and lo! these waters, steeled
By breezeless air to smoothest polish, yield
A vivid repetition of the stars;
Jove—Venus—and the ruddy crest of Mars,
Amid his fellows beauteously revealed
At happy distance from earth's groaning field,
Where ruthless mortals wage incessant wars.
Is it a mirror?—or the nether sphere
Opening to view the abyss in which it feeds
Its own calm fires?—But list! a voice is near;
Great Pan himself low-whispering through the reeds,
"Be thankful, thou; for, if unholy deeds
Ravage the world, tranquillity is here!"

# WILLIAM WORDSWORTH

**Sonnet:** *Composed While the Author Was Writ-*
   *ing a Tract Occasioned by the Convention of Cintra*

I dropped my pen;—and listened to the wind
That sang of trees uptorn and vessels tost;
A midnight harmony, and wholly lost
To the general sense of men by chains confined
Of business, care, or pleasure,—or resigned
To timely sleep. Thought I, the impassioned strain,
Which, without aid of numbers, I sustain,
Like acceptation from the World will find.
Yet some with apprehensive ear shall drink
A dirge devoutly breathed o'er sorrows past,
And to the attendant promise will give heed—
The prophecy,—like that of this wild blast,
Which, while it makes the heart with sadness shrink,
Tells also of bright calms that shall succeed.

# WILLIAM WORDSWORTH

*Sonnet: The French and the Spanish Guerillas*

Hunger, and sultry heat, and nipping blast
From bleak hill-top, and length of march by night.
Through heavy swamp, or over snow-clad height,
These hardships ill sustained, these dangers past,
The roving Spanish Bands are reached at last,
Charged, and dispersed like foam: but as a flight
Of scattered quails by signs do reunite,
So these,—and, heard of once again, are chased
With combinations of long-practised art
And newly-kindled hope; but they are fled,
Gone are they, viewless as the buried dead;
Where now?—Their sword is at the Foeman's heart!
And thus from year to year his walk they thwart,
And hang like dreams around his guilty bed.

# WILLIAM WORDSWORTH

*Sonnet: To——*

Happy the feeling from the bosom thrown
In perfect shape whose beauty Time shall spare
Though a breath made it, like a bubble blown
For summer pastime into wanton air;
Happy the thought best likened to a stone
Of the sea-beach, when, polished with nice care,
Veins it discovers exquisite and rare,
Which for the loss of that moist gleam atone
That tempted first to gather it. O chief
Of Friends! such feelings if I here present,
Such thoughts, with others mixed less fortunate;
Then smile into my heart a fond belief
That Thou, if not with partial joy elate,
Receiv'st the gift for more than mild content!

# WILLIAM WORDSWORTH

*onnet: The Wild Duck's Nest*

The Imperial Consort of the Fairy King
Owns not a sylvan bower; or gorgeous cell
With emerald floored, and with purpureal shell
Ceilinged and roofed; that is so fair a thing
As this low structure—for the tasks of Spring
Prepared by one who loves the buoyant swell
Of the brisk waves, yet here consents to dwell;
And spreads in steadfast peace her brooding wing.
Words cannot paint the o'ershadowing yew-tree bough,
And dimly-gleaming nest,—a hollow crown
Of golden leaves inlaid with silver down,
Fine as the Mother's softest plumes allow:
I gaze—and almost wish to lay aside
Humanity, weak slave of cumbrous pride!

# WILLIAM WORDSWORTH

*Sonnet: Surprised by Joy*

Surprised by joy—impatient as the wind
I turned to share the transport—Oh! with whom
But Thee, deep buried in the silent Tomb,
That spot which no vicissitude can find?
Love, faithful love, recalled thee to my mind—
But how could I forget thee? —Through what power,
Even for the least division of an hour,
Have I been so beguiled as to be blind
To my most grievous loss? —That thought's return
Was the worst pang that sorrow ever bore,
Save one, one only, when I stood forlorn,
Knowing my heart's best treasure was no more;
That neither present time, nor years unborn
Could to my sight that heavenly face restore.

# WILLIAM WORDSWORTH

Sonnet: *It Is a Beauteous Evening*

It is a beauteous Evening, calm and free;
The holy time is quiet as a Nun
Breathless with adoration; the broad sun
Is sinking down in its tranquillity;
The gentleness of heaven is on the Sea;
Listen! the mighty Being is awake,
And doth with his eternal motion make
A sound like thunder—everlastingly.
Dear Child! dear Girl! that walkest with me here,
If thou appear'st untouched by solemn thought,
Thy nature is not therefore less divine:
Thou liest in Abraham's bosom all the year;
And worshipp'st at the Temple's inner shrine,
God being with thee when we know it not.

# WILLIAM WORDSWORTH

## Sonnet: *Where Lies the Land*

Where lies the Land to which yon Ship must go?
Festively she puts forth in trim array;
As vigorous as a Lark at break of day:
Is she for tropic suns, or polar snow?
What boots the inquiry? —Neither friend nor foe
She cares for; let her travel where she may,
She finds familiar names, a beaten way
Ever before her, and a wind to blow.
Yet still I ask, what Haven is her mark?
And, almost as it was when ships were rare,
(From time to time, like Pilgrims, here and there
Crossing the waters) doubt, and something dark,
Of the old Sea some reverential fear,
Is with me at thy farewell, joyous Bark!

# WILLIAM WORDSWORTH

onnet: *The World Is Too Much with Us*

The world is too much with us; late and soon,
Getting and spending, we lay waste our powers:
Little we see in Nature that is ours;
We have given our hearts away, a sordid boon!
This Sea that bares her bosom to the moon;
The Winds that will be howling at all hours,
And are up-gathered now like sleeping flowers;
For this, for every thing, we are out of tune;
It moves us not. —Great God! I'd rather be
A Pagan suckled in a creed outworn;
So might I, standing on this pleasant lea,
Have glimpses that would make me less forlorn;
Have sight of Proteus rising from the sea;
Or hear old Triton blow his wreathèd horn.

## Sonnet: September, 1815

While not a leaf seems faded,—while the fields,
With ripening harvest prodigally fair,
In brightest sunshine bask,—this nipping air,
Sent from some distant clime where Winter wields
His icy scimitar, a foretaste yields
Of bitter change—and bids the Flowers beware;
And whispers to the silent Birds, "Prepare
Against the threatening Foe your trustiest shields."
For me, who under kindlier laws belong
To Nature's tuneful quire, this rustling dry
Through leaves yet green, and yon crystalline sky,
Announce a season potent to renew,
Mid frost and snow, the instinctive joys of song,
And nobler cares than listless summer knew.

# WILLIAM WORDSWORTH

## Sonnet: *To the Lady Beaumont*

Lady! the songs of Spring were in the grove
While I was shaping beds for winter flowers;
While I was planting green unfading bowers,
And shrubs to hang upon the warm alcove,
And sheltering wall; and still, as fancy wove
The dream, to time and nature's blended powers
I gave this paradise for winter hours,
A labyrinth, Lady! which your feet shall rove.
Yes! when the sun of life more feebly shines,
Becoming thoughts, I trust, of solemn gloom
Or of high gladness you shall hither bring;
And these perennial bowers and murmuring pines
Be gracious as the music and the bloom
And all the mighty ravishment of spring.

# WILLIAM WORDSWORTH

*Sonnet: Composed after a Journey across the Hamilton Hills,*
    *Yorkshire*

> Dark and more dark the shades of evening fell;
> The wished-for point was reached, but late the hour;
> And little could be gained from all that dower
> Of prospect, whereof many thousands tell.
> Yet did the glowing west in all its power
> Salute us;—there stood Indian Citadel,
> Temple of Greece, and Minster with its tower
> Substantially expressed—a place for Bell
> Or Clock to toll from. Many a tempting Isle,
> With Groves that never were imagined, lay
> Mid Seas how steadfast! objects all for the eye
> Of silent rapture; but we felt the while
> We should forget them; they are of the sky,
> And from our earthly memory fade away.

## Love

All thoughts, all passions, all delights,
Whatever stirs this mortal frame,
All are but ministers of Love,
   And feed his sacred flame.

Oft in my waking dreams do I
Live o'er again that happy hour,
When midway on the mount I lay,
   Beside the ruined tower.

The moonshine, stealing o'er the scene,
Had blended with the lights of eve;
And she was there, my hope, my joy,
   My own dear Genevieve!

She leaned against the armed man,
The statue of the armed knight;
She stood and listened to my lay,
   Amid the lingering light.

Few sorrows hath she of her own,
My hope! my joy! my Genevieve!
She loves me best, whene'er I sing
   The songs that make her grieve.

I played a soft and doleful air,
I sang an old and moving story—
An old rude song, that suited well
   That ruin wild and hoary.

She listened with a flitting blush,
With downcast eyes and modest grace;
For well she knew, I could not choose
   But gaze upon her face.

I told her of the knight that wore
Upon his shield a burning brand;
And that for ten long years he wooed
   The Lady of the Land.

I told her how he pined; and ah!
The deep, the low, the pleading tone
With which I sang another's love,
   Interpreted my own.

She listened with a flitting blush,
With downcast eyes and modest grace;
And she forgave me, that I gazed
   Too fondly on her face.

But when I told the cruel scorn
That crazed that bold and lovely Knight,
And that he crossed the mountain-woods,
   Nor rested day nor night;

That sometimes from the savage den,
And sometimes from the darksome shade,
And sometimes starting up at once
   In green and sunny glade,—

There came and looked him in the face
An angel beautiful and bright;
And that he knew it was a Fiend,
  The miserable Knight!

And that unknowing what he did,
He leaped amid a murderous band,
And saved from outrage worse than death
  The Lady of the Land;—

And how she wept, and clasped his knees;
And how she tended him in vain—
And ever strove to expiate
  The scorn that crazed his brain;—

And that she nursed him in a cave;
And how his madness went away,
When on the yellow forest leaves
  A dying man he lay;—

His dying words—but when he reached
That tenderest strain of all the ditty,
My faltering voice and pausing harp
  Disturbed her soul with pity!

All impulses of soul and sense
Had thrilled my guileless Genevieve;
The music, and the doleful tale,
  The rich and balmy eve;

And hopes, and fears that kindle hope,
An undistinguishable throng,
And gentle wishes, long subdued,
  Subdued and cherished long!

SAMUEL TAYLOR COLERIDGE

She wept with pity and delight,
She blushed with love, and virgin shame;
And like the murmur of a dream,
   I heard her breathe my name.

Her bosom heaved—she stept aside,
As conscious of my look she stept—
Then suddenly, with timorous eye
   She fled to me and wept.

She half enclosed me with her arms,
She pressed me with a meek embrace;
And bending back her head, looked up,
   And gazed upon my face.

'Twas partly love, and partly fear,
And partly 'twas a bashful art,
That I might rather feel, than see
   The swelling of her heart.

I calmed her fears, and she was calm,
And told her love with virgin-pride;
And so I won my Genevieve,
   My bright and beauteous Bride.

# SAMUEL TAYLOR COLERIDGE

## Kubla Khan

In Xanadu did Kubla Khan
A stately pleasure-dome decree:
Where Alph, the sacred river, ran
Through caverns measureless to man
   Down to a sunless sea.
So twice five miles of fertile ground
With walls and towers were girdled round:
And there were gardens bright with sinuous rills,
Where blossomed many an incense-bearing tree;
And here were forests ancient as the hills,
Enfolding sunny spots of greenery.

But oh! that deep romantic chasm which slanted
Down the green hill athwart a cedarn cover!
A savage place! as holy and enchanted
As e'er beneath a waning moon was haunted
By woman wailing for her demon-lover!
And from this chasm, with ceaseless turmoil seething,
As if this earth in fast thick pants were breathing,
A mighty fountain momently was forced:
Amid whose swift half-intermitted burst
Huge fragments vaulted like rebounding hail,
Or chaffy grain beneath the thresher's flail:
And 'mid these dancing rocks at once and ever
It flung up momently the sacred river.

Five miles meandering with a mazy motion
Through wood and dale the sacred river ran,
Then reached the caverns measureless to man,
And sank in tumult to a lifeless ocean:
And 'mid this tumult Kubla heard from far
Ancestral voices prophesying war!
    The shadow of the dome of pleasure
    Floated midway on the waves;
    Where was heard the mingled measure
    From the fountain and the caves.
It was a miracle of rare device,
A sunny pleasure-dome with caves of ice!

    A damsel with a dulcimer
    In a vision once I saw:
    It was an Abyssinian maid,
    And on her dulcimer she played,
    Singing of Mount Abora.
    Could I revive within me
    Her symphony and song,
    To such a deep delight 'twould win me,
That with music loud and long,
I would build that dome in air,
That sunny dome! those caves of ice!
And all who heard should see them there,
And all should cry, Beware! Beware!
His flashing eyes, his floating hair!
Weave a circle round him thrice,
And close your eyes with holy dread,
For he on honey-dew hath fed,
And drunk the milk of Paradise.

# SAMUEL TAYLOR COLERIDGE

## The Rime of the Ancient Mariner

### Part I

It is an ancient Mariner,
And he stoppeth one of three.
"By thy long grey beard and glittering eye,
Now wherefore stopp'st thou me?

The Bridegroom's doors are opened wide,
And I am next of kin;
The guests are met, the feast is set:
May'st hear the merry din."

He holds him with his skinny hand,
"There was a ship," quoth he.
"Hold off! unhand me, grey-beard loon!"
Eftsoons his hand dropt he.

He holds him with his glittering eye—
The Wedding-Guest stood still,
And listens like a three years' child:
The Mariner hath his will.

The Wedding-Guest sat on a stone:
He cannot choose but hear;
And thus spake on that ancient man,
The bright-eyed Mariner.

# SAMUEL TAYLOR COLERIDGE

"The ship was cheered, the harbour cleared,
Merrily did we drop
Below the kirk, below the hill,
Below the lighthouse top.

The Sun came up upon the left,
Out of the sea came he!
And he shone bright, and on the right
Went down into the sea.

Higher and higher every day,
Till over the mast at noon—"
The Wedding-Guest here beat his breast,
For he heard the loud bassoon.

The bride hath paced into the hall,
Red as a rose is she;
Nodding their heads before her goes
The merry minstrelsy.

The Wedding-Guest he beat his breast,
Yet he cannot choose but hear;
And thus spake on that ancient man,
The bright-eyed Mariner.

"And now the Storm-blast came, and he
Was tyrannous and strong:
He struck with his o'ertaking wings,
And chased us south along.

With sloping mast and dipping prow,
As who pursued with yell and blow
Still treads the shadow of his foe,
And forward bends his head,
The ship drove fast, loud roared the blast,
And southward aye we fled.

And now there came both mist and snow,
And it grew wondrous cold:
And ice, mast-high, came floating by,
As green as emerald.

And through the drifts the snowy clifts
Did send a dismal sheen:
Nor shapes of men nor beasts we ken—
The ice was all between.

The ice was here, the ice was there,
The ice was all around:
It cracked and growled, and roared and howled,
Like noises in a swound!

At length did cross an Albatross,
Thorough the fog it came;
As if it had been a Christian soul,
We hailed it in God's name.

It ate the food it ne'er had eat,
And round and round it flew.
The ice did split with a thunder-fit;
The helmsman steered us through!

[129

And a good south wind sprung up behind;
The Albatross did follow,
And every day, for food or play,
Came to the mariner's hollo!

In mist or cloud, on mast or shroud,
It perched for vespers nine;
Whiles all the night, through fog-smoke white,
Glimmered the white Moon-shine."

"God save thee, ancient Mariner!
From the fiends, that plague thee thus!—
Why look'st thou so?" —"With my cross-bow
I shot the Albatross.

## Part II

The Sun now rose upon the right:
Out of the sea came he,
Still hid in mist, and on the left
Went down into the sea.

And the good south wind still blew behind,
But no sweet bird did follow,
Nor any day for food or play
Came to the mariner's hollo!

And I had done a hellish thing,
And it would work 'em woe:
For all averred, I had killed the bird
That made the breeze to blow.
Ah wretch! said they, the bird to slay,
That made the breeze to blow!

Nor dim nor red, like God's own head,
The glorious Sun uprist:
Then all averred, I had killed the bird
That brought the fog and mist.
'Twas right, said they, such birds to slay,
That bring the fog and mist.

The fair breeze blew, the white foam flew,
The furrow followed free;
We were the first that ever burst
Into that silent sea.

Down dropt the breeze, the sails dropt down,
'Twas sad as sad could be;
And we did speak only to break
The silence of the sea!

All in a hot and copper sky,
The bloody Sun, at noon,
Right up above the mast did stand,
No bigger than the Moon.

Day after day, day after day,
We stuck, nor breath nor motion
As idle as a painted ship
Upon a painted ocean.

Water, water, every where,
And all the boards did shrink;
Water, water, every where,
Nor any drop to drink.

The very deep did rot: O Christ!
That ever this should be!
Yea, slimy things did crawl with legs
Upon the slimy sea.

About, about, in reel and rout
The death-fires danced at night;
The water, like a witch's oils,
Burnt green, and blue and white.

And some in dreams assured were
Of the Spirit that plagued us so;
Nine fathom deep he had followed us
From the land of mist and snow.

And every tongue, through utter drought,
Was withered at the root;
We could not speak, no more than if
We had been choked with soot.

Ah! well a-day! what evil looks
Had I from old and young!
Instead of the cross, the Albatross
About my neck was hung.

## Part III

There passed a weary time. Each throat
Was parched, and glazed each eye,
A weary time! a weary time!
How glazed each weary eye,
When looking westward, I beheld
A something in the sky.

At first it seemed a little speck,
And then it seemed a mist;
It moved and moved, and took at last
A certain shape, I wist.

A speck, a mist, a shape, I wist!
And still it neared and neared:
As if it dodged a water-sprite,
It plunged and tacked and veered.

With throats unslaked, with black lips baked,
We could nor laugh nor wail;
Through utter drought all dumb we stood!
I bit my arm, I sucked my blood,
And cried, A sail! a sail!

With throats unslaked, with black lips baked,
Agape they heard me call:
Gramercy! they for joy did grin,
And all at once their breath drew in,
As they were drinking all.

See! see! (I cried) she tacks no more!
Hither to work us weal;
Without a breeze, without a tide,
She steadies with upright keel!

The western wave was all a-flame.
The day was well nigh done!
Almost upon the western wave
Rested the broad bright Sun;
When that strange shape drove suddenly
Betwixt us and the Sun.

And straight the Sun was flecked with bars,
(Heaven's Mother send us grace!)
As if through a dungeon-grate he peered
With broad and burning face.

Alas! (thought I, and my heart beat loud)
How fast she nears and nears!
Are those *her* sails that glance in the Sun,
Like restless gossameres?

Are those *her* ribs through which the Sun
Did peer, as through a grate?
And is that Woman all her crew?
Is that a DEATH? and are there two?
Is DEATH that woman's mate?

*Her* lips were red, *her* looks were free,
Her locks were yellow as gold:
Her skin was as white as leprosy,
The Night-mare LIFE-IN-DEATH was she,
Who thicks man's blood with cold.

The naked hulk alongside came,
And the twain were casting dice;
'The game is done! I've won! I've won!'
Quoth she, and whistles thrice.

The Sun's rim dips; the stars rush out:
At one stride comes the dark;
With far-heard whisper, o'er the sea,
Off shot the spectre-bark.

We listened and looked sideways up!
Fear at my heart, as at a cup,
My life-blood seemed to sip!
The stars were dim, and thick the night,
The steersman's face by his lamp gleamed white;
From the sails the dew did drip—
Till clomb above the eastern bar
The horned Moon, with one bright star
Within the nether tip.

One after one, by the star-dogged Moon,
Too quick for groan or sigh,
Each turned his face with a ghastly pang,
And cursed me with his eye.

Four times fifty living men,
(And I heard nor sigh nor groan)
With heavy thump, a lifeless lump,
They dropped down one by one

The souls did from their bodies fly,—
They fled to bliss or woe!
And every soul, it passed me by,
Like the whizz of my cross-bow!"

Part IV

"I fear thee, ancient Mariner!
I fear thy skinny hand!
And thou art long, and lank, and brown,
As is the ribbed sea-sand.

I fear thee and thy glittering eye,
And thy skinny hand so brown."—
"Fear not, fear not, thou Wedding-Guest!
This body dropt not down.

Alone, alone, all, all alone,
Alone on a wide wide sea!
And never a saint took pity on
My soul in agony.

The many men, so beautiful!
And they all dead did lie:
And a thousand thousand slimy things
Lived on; and so did I.

I looked upon the rotting sea,
And drew my eyes away;
I looked upon the rotting deck,
And there the dead men lay.

I looked to heaven, and tried to pray;
But or ever a prayer had gusht,
A wicked whisper came, and made
My heart as dry as dust.

I closed my lids, and kept them close,
And the balls like pulses beat;
For the sky and the sea, and the sea and the sky
Lay like a load on my weary eye.
And the dead were at my feet.

The cold sweat melted from their limbs,
Nor rot nor reek did they:
The look with which they looked on me
Had never passed away.

An orphan's curse would drag to hell
A spirit from on high;
But oh! more horrible than that
Is the curse in the dead man's eye!
Seven days, seven nights, I saw that curse,
And yet I could not die.

The moving Moon went up the sky,
And no where did abide:
Softly she was going up,
And a star or two beside—

Her beams bemocked the sultry main,
Like April hoar-frost spread;
But where the ship's huge shadow lay,
The charmèd water burnt alway
A still and awful red.

Beyond the shadow of the ship,
I watched the water-snakes:
They moved in tracks of shining white,
And when they reared, the elfish light
Fell off in hoary flakes.

Within the shadow of the ship
I watched their rich attire:
Blue, glossy green, and velvet black,
They coiled and swam; and every track
Was a flash of golden fire.

# SAMUEL TAYLOR COLERIDGE

O happy living things! no tongue
Their beauty might declare:
A spring of love gushed from my heart,
And I blessed them unaware:
Sure my kind saint took pity on me,
And I blessed them unaware.

The self-same moment I could pray;
And from my neck so free
The Albatross fell off, and sank
Like lead into the sea.

### Part V

Oh sleep! it is a gentle thing,
Beloved from pole to pole!
To Mary Queen the praise be given!
She sent the gentle sleep from Heaven,
That slid into my soul.

The silly buckets on the deck,
That had so long remained,
I dreamt that they were filled with dew;
And when I awoke, it rained.

My lips were wet, my throat was cold,
My garments all were dank;
Sure I had drunken in my dreams,
And still my body drank.

I moved, and could not feel my limbs:
I was so light—almost
I thought that I had died in sleep,
And was a blessèd ghost.

And soon I heard a roaring wind:
It did not come anear;
But with its sound it shook the sails,
That were so thin and sere.

The upper air burst into life!
And a hundred fire-flags sheen,
To and fro they were hurried about!
And to and fro, and in and out,
The wan stars danced between.

And the coming wind did roar more loud,
And the sails did sigh like sedge;
And the rain poured down from one black cloud;
The Moon was as its edge.

The thick black cloud was cleft, and still
The Moon was at its side:
Like waters shot from some high crag,
The lightning fell with never a jag,
A river steep and wide.

The loud wind never reached the ship,
Yet now the ship moved on!
Beneath the lightning and the Moon
The dead men gave a groan.

They groaned, they stirred, they all uprose,
Nor spake, nor moved their eyes;
It had been strange, even in a dream,
To have seen those dead men rise.

The helmsman steered, the ship moved on;
Yet never a breeze up-blew;
The mariners all 'gan work the ropes,
Where they were wont to do;
They raised their limbs like lifeless tools—
We were a ghastly crew.

The body of my brother's son
Stood by me, knee to knee:
The body and I pulled at one rope,
But he said nought to me."

"I fear thee, ancient Mariner!"
"Be calm, thou Wedding-Guest!
'Twas not those souls that fled in pain,
Which to their corses came again,
But a troop of spirits blest:

For when it dawned—they dropped their arms,
And clustered round the mast;
Sweet sounds rose slowly through their mouths,
And from their bodies passed.

Around, around, flew each sweet sound,
Then darted to the Sun;
Slowly the sounds came back again,
Now mixed, now one by one.

Sometimes a-dropping from the sky
I heard the sky-lark sing;
Sometimes all little birds that are,
How they seemed to fill the sea and air
With their sweet jargoning!

And now 'twas like all instruments,
Now like a lonely flute;
And now it is an angel's song,
That makes the heavens be mute.

It ceased; yet still the sails made on
A pleasant noise till noon,
A noise like of a hidden brook
In the leafy month of June,
That to the sleeping woods all night
Singeth a quiet tune.

Till noon we quietly sailed on,
Yet never a breeze did breathe:
Slowly and smoothly went the ship,
Moved onward from beneath.

Under the keel nine fathom deep,
From the land of mist and snow,
The spirit slid: and it was he
That made the ship to go.
The sails at noon left off their tune,
And the ship stood still also.

The Sun, right up above the mast,
Had fixed her to the ocean:
But in a minute she 'gan stir,
With a short uneasy motion—
Backwards and forwards half her length
With a short uneasy motion.

Then like a pawing horse let go,
She made a sudden bound:
It flung the blood into my head,
And I fell down in a swound.

How long in that same fit I lay,
I have not to declare;
But ere my living life returned,
I heard and in my soul discerned
Two voices in the air.

'Is it he?' quoth one, 'Is this the man?
By him who died on cross,
With his cruel bow he laid full low
The harmless Albatross.

The spirit who bideth by himself
In the land of mist and snow,
He loved the bird that loved the man
Who shot him with his bow.'

The other was a softer voice,
As soft as honey-dew:
Quoth he, 'The man hath penance done,
And penance more will do.'

### Part VI

#### First Voice

'But tell me, tell me! speak again,
Thy soft response renewing—
What makes that ship drive on so fast?
What is the ocean doing?'

# SAMUEL TAYLOR COLERIDGE

### Second Voice

'Still as a slave before his lord,
The ocean hath no blast;
His great bright eye most silently
Up to the Moon is cast—

If he may know which way to go;
For she guides him smooth or grim.
See, brother, see! how graciously
She looketh down on him.'

### First Voice

'But why drives on that ship so fast,
Without or wave or wind?'

### Second Voice

'The air is cut away before,
And closes from behind.

Fly, brother, fly! more high, more high!
Or we shall be belated:
For slow and slow that ship will go,
When the Mariner's trance is abated.'

I woke, and we were sailing on
As in a gentle weather:
'Twas night, calm night, the moon was high;
The dead men stood together.

[143

# SAMUEL TAYLOR COLERIDGE

All stood together on the deck,
For a charnel-dungeon fitter:
All fixed on me their stony eyes,
That in the Moon did glitter.

The pang, the curse, with which they died,
Had never passed away:
I could not draw my eyes from theirs,
Nor turn them up to pray.

And now this spell was snapt: once more
I viewed the ocean green,
And looked far forth, yet little saw
Of what had else been seen—

Like one, that on a lonesome road
Doth walk in fear and dread,
And having once turned round walks on,
And turns no more his head;
Because he knows, a frightful fiend
Doth close behind him tread.

But soon he breathed a wind on me,
Nor sound nor motion made:
Its path was not upon the sea,
In ripple or in shade.

It raised my hair, it fanned my cheek
Like a meadow-gale of spring—
It mingled strangely with my fears,
Yet it felt like a welcoming.

Swiftly, swiftly flew the ship,
Yet he sailed softly too:
Sweetly, sweetly blew the breeze—
On me alone it blew.

Oh! dream of joy! is this indeed
The light-house top I see?
Is this the hill? is this the kirk?
Is this my own countree?

We drifted o'er the harbour-bar,
And I with sobs did pray—
O let me be awake, my God!
Or let me sleep alway.

The harbour-bay was clear as glass,
So smoothly it was strewn!
And on the bay the moonlight lay,
And the shadow of the Moon.

The rock shone bright, the kirk no less.
That stands above the rock:
The moonlight steeped in silentness
The steady weathercock.

And the bay was white with silent light,
Till rising from the same,
Full many shapes, that shadows were,
In crimson colours came.

A little distance from the prow
Those crimson shadows were:
I turned my eyes upon the deck—
Oh, Christ! what saw I there!

Each corse lay flat, lifeless and flat,
And, by the holy rood!
A man all light, a seraph-man,
On every corse there stood.

This seraph-band, each waved his hand:
It was a heavenly sight!
They stood as signals to the land,
Each one a lovely light;

This seraph-band, each waved his hand,
No voice did they impart—
No voice; but oh! the silence sank
Like music on my heart.

But soon I heard the dash of oars,
I heard the Pilot's cheer;
My head was turned perforce away
And I saw a boat appear.

The Pilot and the Pilot's boy,
I heard them coming fast:
Dear Lord in Heaven! it was joy
The dead men could not blast.

I saw a third—I heard his voice:
It is the Hermit good!
He singeth loud his godly hymns
That he makes in the wood.
He'll shrieve my soul, he'll wash away
The Albatross's blood.

Part VII

This Hermit good lives in that wood
Which slopes down to the sea.
How loudly his sweet voice he rears!
He loves to talk with marineres
That come from a far countree.

He kneels at morn, and noon, and eve—
He hath a cushion plump:
It is the moss that wholly hides
The rotted old oak-stump.

The skiff-boat neared: I heard them talk,
'Why, this is strange, I trow!
Where are those lights so many and fair,
That signal made but now?'

'Strange, by my faith!' the Hermit said—
'And they answered not our cheer!
The planks looked warped! and see those sails,
How thin they are and sere!
I never saw aught like to them,
Unless perchance it were

Brown skeletons of leaves that lag
My forest-brook along;
When the ivy-tod is heavy with snow,
And the owlet whoops to the wolf below,
That eats the she-wolf's young.'

'Dear Lord! it hath a fiendish look—
(The Pilot made reply)
I am a-feared'—'Push on, push on!'
Said the Hermit cheerily.

The boat came closer to the ship,
But I not spake nor stirred;
The boat came close beneath the ship,
And straight a sound was heard.

Under the water it rumbled on,
Still louder and more dread:
It reached the ship, it split the bay;
The ship went down like lead.

Stunned by the loud and dreadful sound,
Which sky and ocean smote,
Like one that hath been seven days drowned
My body lay afloat;
But swift as dreams, myself I found
Within the Pilot's boat.

Upon the whirl, where sank the ship,
The boat spun round and round;
And all was still, save that the hill
Was telling of the sound.

I moved my lips—the Pilot shrieked
And fell down in a fit;
The holy Hermit raised his eyes,
And prayed where he did sit.

I took the oars: the Pilot's boy,
Who now doth crazy go,
Laughed loud and long, and all the while
His eyes went to and fro.
'Ha! ha!' quoth he, 'full plain I see,
The Devil knows how to row.'

And now, in my own countree,
I stood on the firm land!
The Hermit stepped forth from the boat,
And scarcely he could stand.

'O shrieve me, shrieve me, holy man!'
The Hermit crossed his brow.
'Say quick,' quoth he, 'I bid thee say—
What manner of man art thou?'

Forthwith this frame of mine was wrenched
With a woful agony,
Which forced me to begin my tale;
And then it left me free.

Since then, at an uncertain hour,
That agony returns:
And till my ghastly tale is told,
This heart within me burns,

I pass, like night, from land to land;
I have strange power to speech;
That moment that his face I see,
I know the man that must hear me:
To him my tale I teach.

[149

What loud uproar burst from that door!
The wedding-guests are there:
But in the garden-bower the bride
And bride-maids singing are:
And hark the little vesper bell,
Which biddeth me to prayer!

O Wedding-Guest! this soul hath been
Alone on a wide wide sea:
So lonely 'twas, that God himself
Scarce seemèd there to be.

O sweeter than the marriage-feast,
'Tis sweeter far to me,
To walk together to the kirk
With a goodly company!—

To walk together to the kirk
And all together pray,
While each to his great Father bends,
Old men, and babes, and loving friends
And youths and maidens gay!

Farewell, farewell! but this I tell
To thee, thou Wedding-Guest!
He prayeth well, who loveth well
Both man and bird and beast.

He prayeth best, who loveth best
All things both great and small;
For the dear God who loveth us,
He made and loveth all."

SAMUEL TAYLOR COLERIDGE

The Mariner, whose eye is bright,
Whose beard with age is hoar,
Is gone: and now the Wedding-Guest
Turned from the bridegroom's door.

He went like one that hath been stunned,
And is of sense forlorn:
A sadder and a wiser man,
He rose the morrow morn.

# SAMUEL TAYLOR COLERIDGE

*Recollections of Love*

## I

How warm this woodland wild Recess!
  Love surely hath been breathing here.
  And this sweet bed of heath, my dear!
Swells up, then sinks with faint caress,
  As if to have you yet more near.

## II

Eight springs have flown, since last I lay
  On sea-ward Quantock's heathy hills,
  Where quiet sounds from hidden rills
Float here and there, like things astray,
  And high o'er head the sky-lark shrills.

## III

No voice as yet had made the air
  Be music with your name: yet why
  That asking look? That yearning sigh?
That sense of promise every where?
  Beloved! flew your spirit by?

## IV

As when a mother doth explore
  The rose-mark on her long lost child,
  I met, I lov'd you, maiden mild!
As whom I long had lov'd before—
  So deeply had I been beguil'd.

### V

You stood before me like a thought,
   A dream remember'd in a dream.
   But when those meek eyes first did seem
To tell me, Love within you wrought—
   O Greta, dear domestic stream!

### VI

Has not, since then, Love's prompture deep,
   Has not Love's whisper evermore,
   Been ceaseless, as thy gentle roar?
Sole voice, when other voices sleep,
   Dear under-song in Clamor's hour.

[From] *The Three Graves*

So gentle Ellen now no more
   Could make this sad house cheary;
And Mary's melancholy ways
   Drove Edward wild and weary.

Lingering he rais'd his latch at eve,
   Though tired in heart and limb:
He lov'd no other place, and yet
   Home was no home to him.

One evening he took up a book,
   And nothing in it read;
Then flung it down, and groaning cried,
   Oh! Heaven! that I were dead.

Mary look'd up into his face,
   And nothing to him said;
She tried to smile, and on his arm
   Mournfully leaned her head.

And he burst into tears, and fell
   Upon his knees in prayer:
Her heart is broke! O God! my grief,
   It is too great to bear!

'Twas such a foggy time as makes
   Old Sextons, Sir! like me,
Rest on their spades to cough; the spring
   Was late uncommonly.


And then the hot days, all at once,
   They came, we knew not how:
You look'd about for shade, when scarce
   A leaf was on a bough.


It happen'd then ('twas in the bower
   A furlong up the wood:
Perhaps you know the place, and yet
   I scarce know how you shou'd)


No path leads thither, 'tis not nigh
   To any pasture-plot;
But cluster'd near the chattering brook,
   Lone hollies mark'd the spot.


Those hollies of themselves a shape
   As of an arbor took,
A close, round arbor; and it stands
   Not three strides from a brook.


Within this arbor, which was still
   With scarlet berries hung,
Were these three friends, one Sunday morn,
   Just as the first bell rung.

[155

# SAMUEL TAYLOR COLERIDGE

'Tis sweet to hear a brook, 'tis sweet
　　To hear the Sabbath-bell,
'Tis sweet to hear them both at once,
　　Deep in a woody dell.

His limbs along the moss, his head
　　Upon a mossy heap,
With shut-up senses, Edward lay:
That brook e'en on a working day
　　Might chatter one to sleep.

And he had pass'd a restless night,
　　And was not well in health;
The women sat down by his side,
　　And talk'd as 'twere by stealth.

"The Sun peeps thro' the close thick leaves,
　　"See, dearest Ellen! see!
" 'Tis in the leaves, a little Sun,
　　"No bigger than your ee;

"A tiny Sun, and it has got
　　"A perfect glory too:
"Ten thousand threads and hairs of light,
"Make up a glory, gay and bright,
　　"Round that small orb, so blue."

And then they argued of those rays,
　　What colour they might be:
Says this, "they're mostly green"; says that,
　　"They're amber-like to me."

156]

So they sat chatting, while bad thoughts,
   Were troubling Edward's rest;
But soon they heard his heart quick pants,
   And the thumping in his breast.

"A Mother, too!" these self-same words
   Did Edward mutter plain;
His face was drawn back on itself,
   With horror and huge pain.

Both groan'd at once, for both knew well
   What thoughts were in his mind;
When he wak'd up, and star'd like one
   That hath been just struck blind.

He sat upright; and ere the dream
   Had had time to depart,
"O God, forgive me! (he exclaim'd)
   "I have torn out her heart."

Then Ellen shriek'd, and forthwith burst
   Into ungentle laughter;
And Mary shiver'd, where she sat,
   And never she smil'd after.

# SAMUEL TAYLOR COLERIDGE

[From] *To a Young Friend*

And haply, bason'd in some unsunn'd cleft,
A beauteous spring, the rocks' collected tears,
Sleeps shelter'd there, scarce wrinkled by the gale!

# SAMUEL TAYLOR COLERIDGE

Sonnet: *To the River Otter*

Dear native Brook! wild Streamlet of the West!
　How many various-fated years have past,
　What happy, and what mournful hours, since last
I skimm'd the smooth thin stone along thy breast,
Numbering its light leaps! yet so deep impresst
Sink the sweet scenes of childhood, that mine eyes
　I never shut amid the sunny ray,
But strait with all their tints thy waters rise,
　Thy crossing plank, thy marge with willows grey,
And bedded sand that vein'd with various dyes
Gleam'd through thy bright transparence! On my way,
　Visions of childhood! oft have ye beguiled
Lone manhood's cares, yet waking fondest sighs.
　Ah! that I were once more a careless child!

# SAMUEL TAYLOR COLERIDGE

*Sonnet: Oft o'er My Brain*

Oft o'er my brain does that strange fancy roll
Which makes the present (while the flesh doth last)
Seem a mere semblance of some unknown past,
Mix'd with such feelings, as perplex the soul
Self-question'd in her sleep: and some have said
   We liv'd, ere yet this robe of Flesh we wore.
   O my sweet baby! when I reach my door,
If heavy looks should tell me thou art dead
(As sometimes, thro' excess of hope, I fear)
I think, that I should struggle to believe
   Thou wert a spirit, to this nether sphere
Sentenc'd for some more venial crime to grieve;
Did'st scream, then spring to meet Heaven's quic
    reprieve,
   While we wept idly o'er thy little bier!

Human Life

On the Denial of Immortality

A Fragment

If dead, we cease to be; if total gloom
    Swallow up life's brief flash for aye, we fare
As summer-gusts, of sudden birth and doom,
    Whose sound and motion not alone declare,
But are their whole of being! If the Breath
    Be Life itself, and not its Task and Tent,
If ev'n a soul like Milton's can know death;
    O Man! thou vessel purposeless, unmeant,
Yet drone-hive strange of phantom purposes,
    Surplus of nature's dread activity,
Which, as she gaz'd on some nigh-finish'd vase,
Retreating slow, with meditative pause,
    She form'd with restless hands unconsciously.
Blank accident! nothing's anomaly!
    If rootless thus, thus substanceless thy state,
Go, weigh thy dreams, and be thy Hopes thy Fears,
The counter-weights!—Thy Laughter and thy Tears
    Mean but themselves, each fittest to create
And to repay the other! Why rejoices
    Thy heart with hollow joy for hollow good,

SAMUEL TAYLOR COLERIDGE

Why cowl thy face beneath the Mourner's hood,
Why waste thy sighs, and thy lamenting voices,
Image of Image, Ghost of Ghostly Elf,
That such a thing, as thou, feel'st warm or cold!
Yet what and whence thy gain, if thou withhold
These costless shadows of thy shadowy self.
Be sad! be glad! be neither! seek, or shun!
Thou hast no reason why! Thou can'st have none!
Thy being's being is contradiction.

# SAMUEL TAYLOR COLERIDGE

From] *The Destiny of Nations*

"Even so" (the exulting Maiden said)
"The sainted Heralds of Good Tidings fell,
"And thus they witness'd God! But now the clouds
"Treading, and storms beneath their feet, they soar
"Higher, and higher soar, and soaring sing
"Loud songs of Triumph! O ye spirits of God,
"Hover around my mortal agonies!"
She spake, and instantly faint melody
Melts on her ear, soothing and sad, and slow,
Such measures, as at calmest midnight heard
By aged Hermit in his holy dream,
Foretell and solace death; and now they rise
Louder, as when with harp and mingled voice
The white-robed multitude of slaughter'd saints
At Heaven's wide-open'd portals gratulant
Receive some martyr'd Patriot. The harmony
Entranced the Maid, till each suspended sense
Brief slumber seized, and confused extacy.

At length awakening slow, she gazed around:
And thro' a Mist, the relict of that trance,
Still thinning as she gaz'd, an Isle appear'd,
Its high, o'erhanging, white, broad-breasted cliffs
Glass'd on the subject ocean. A vast plain
Stretch'd opposite, where ever and anon

The Plough-man following sad his meagre team
Turn'd up fresh sculls unstartled, and the bones
Of fierce hate-breathing combatants, who there
All mingled lay beneath the common earth,
Death's gloomy reconcilement! O'er the Fields
Stept a fair form, repairing all she might,
Her temples olive-wreath'd; and where she trod,
Fresh flowrets rose, and many a foodful herb.
But wan her cheek, her footsteps insecure,
And anxious pleasure beam'd in her faint eye,
As she had newly left a couch of pain,
Pale Convalescent! (Yet some time to rule
With power exclusive o'er the willing world,
That blest prophetic mandate then fulfill'd,
PEACE be on Earth!) An happy while, but brief,
She seem'd to wander with assiduous feet,
And heal'd the recent harm of chill and blight,
And nurs'd each plant that fair and virtuous grew.

But soon a deep precursive sound moan'd hollow:
Black rose the clouds, and now, (as in a dream)
Their reddening shapes, transform'd to Warrior-hosts,
Cours'd o'er the Sky, and battled in mid-air.
Nor did not the large blood-drops fall from Heaven
Portentous! while aloft were seen to float,
Like hideous features blended with the clouds,
Wan Stains of ominous Light! Resign'd, yet sad,
The fair Form bow'd her olive-crowned Brow:
Then o'er the plain with oft reverted eye
Fled till a Place of Tombs she reach'd, and there

Within a ruin'd Sepulchre obscure
Found Hiding-place.

.    .    .    .    .    .    .    .    .

.    .    .    .    .    .    .    .    .

        And first a Landscape rose,
More wild, and waste, and desolate, than where
The white bear, drifting on a field of ice,
Howls to her sundered cubs with piteous rage
And savage agony.

# GEORGE GORDON BYRON

## Newstead Abbey

### 1

In the dome of my Sires as the clear moonbeam falls
Through Silence and Shade o'er its desolate walls,
It shines from afar like the glories of old;
It gilds, but it warms not—'tis dazzling, but cold.

### 2

Let the Sunbeam be bright for the younger of days:
'Tis the light that should shine on a race that decays,
When the Stars are on high and the dew's on the groun
And the long shadow lingers the ruin around.

### 3

And the step that o'erechoes the gray floor of stone
Falls sullenly now, for 'tis only my own;
And sunk are the voices that sounded in mirth,
And empty the goblet, and dreary the hearth.

### 4

And vain was each effort to raise and recall
The brightness of old to illumine our Hall;
And vain was the hope to avert our decline,
And the fate of my fathers had faded to mine.

5

And theirs was the wealth and the fulness of Fame,
And mine to inherit too haughty a name;
And theirs were the times and the triumphs of yore,
And mine to regret, but renew them no more.

6

And Ruin is fixed on my tower and my wall,
Too hoary to fade, and too massy to fall;
It tells not of Time's or the tempest's decay,
But the wreck of the line that have held it in sway.

# GEORGE GORDON BYRON

*She Walks in Beauty*

### I

She walks in Beauty, like the night
   Of cloudless climes and starry skies;
And all that's best of dark and bright
   Meet in her aspect and her eyes:
Thus mellowed to that tender light
   Which Heaven to gaudy day denies.

### II

One shade the more, one ray the less,
   Had half impaired the nameless grace
Which was in every raven tress,
   Or softly lightens o'er her face;
Where thoughts serenely sweet express,
   How pure, how dear their dwelling-place.

### III

And on that cheek, and o'er that brow,
   So soft, so calm, yet eloquent,
The smiles that win, the tints that glow,
   But tell of days in goodness spent,
A mind at peace with all below,
   A heart whose love is innocent!

*When We Two Parted*

### 1

When we two parted
  In silence and tears,
Half broken-hearted
  To sever for years,
Pale grew thy cheek and cold,
  Colder thy kiss;
Truly that hour foretold
  Sorrow to this.

### 2

The dew of the morning
  Sunk chill on my brow—
It felt like the warning
  Of what I feel now.
Thy vows are all broken,
  And light is thy fame:
I hear thy name spoken,
  And share in its shame.

### 3

They name thee before me,
  A knell to mine ear;
A shudder comes o'er me—
  Why wert thou so dear?

They know not I knew thee,
    Who knew thee too well:—
Long, long shall I rue thee,
    Too deeply to tell.

### 4

In secret we met—
    In silence I grieve,
That thy heart could forget,
    Thy spirit deceive.
If I should meet thee
    After long years,
How should I greet thee?—
    With silence and tears.

*Stanzas* for Music

### 1

There be none of Beauty's daughters
   With a magic like thee;
And like music on the waters
   Is thy sweet voice to me:
When, as if its sound were causing
The charmèd Ocean's pausing,
The waves lie still and gleaming,
And the lulled winds seem dreaming:

### 2

And the midnight Moon is weaving
   Her bright chain o'er the deep;
Whose breast is gently heaving,
   As an infant's asleep:
So the spirit bows before thee,
To listen and adore thee;
With a full but soft emotion,
Like the swell of summer's ocean.

# GEORGE GORDON BYRON

## On Jordan's Bank

### I

On Jordan's banks the Arab's camels stray,
On Sion's hill the False One's votaries pray,
The Baal-adorer bows on Sinai's steep—
Yet there—even there—Oh God! thy thunders sleep:

### II

There—where thy finger scorched the tablet stone!
There—where thy shadow to thy people shone!
Thy glory shrouded in its garb of fire:
Thyself—none living see and not expire!

### III

Oh! in the lightning let thy glance appear;
Sweep from his shivered hand the oppressor's spear!
How long by tyrants shall thy land be trod?
How long thy temple worshipless, Oh God?

# GEORGE GORDON BYRON

## The Dream

### I

Our life is two-fold: Sleep hath its own world,
A boundary between the things misnamed
Death and existence: Sleep hath its own world,
And a wide realm of wild reality.
And dreams in their development have breath,
And tears, and tortures, and the touch of joy;
They have a weight upon our waking thoughts,
They take a weight from off our waking toils,
They do divide our being; they become
A portion of ourselves as of our time,
And look like heralds of eternity;
They pass like spirits of the past,—they speak
Like Sybils of the future: they have power—
The tyranny of pleasure and of pain;
They make us what we were not—what they will,
And shake us with the vision that's gone by,
The dread of vanish'd shadows—Are they so?
Is not the past all shadow?—What are they?
Creations of the mind?—The mind can make
Substance, and people planets of its own
With beings brighter than have been, and give
A breath to forms which can outlive all flesh.
I would recall a vision which I dream'd

# GEORGE GORDON BYRON

Perchance in sleep—for in itself a thought,
A slumbering thought, is capable of years,
And curdles a long life into one hour.

## II

I saw two beings in the hues of youth
Standing upon a hill, a gentle hill,
Green, and of mild declivity, the last
As 't were the cape of a long ridge of such,
Save that there was no sea to lave its base,
But a most living landscape, and the wave
Of woods and cornfields, and the abodes of men
Scatter'd at intervals, and wreathing smoke
Arising from such rustic roofs;—the hill
Was crown'd with a peculiar diadem
Of trees, in circular array, so fix'd,
Not by the sport of nature, but of man:
These two, a maiden and a youth, were there
Gazing—the one on all that was beneath
Fair as herself—but the boy gazed on her;
And both were young, and one was beautiful:
And both were young—yet not alike in youth.
As the sweet moon on the horizon's verge,
The maid was on the eve of womanhood;
The boy had fewer summers, but his heart
Had far outgrown his years, and to his eye
There was but one beloved face on earth,
And that was shining on him: he had look'd
Upon it till it could not pass away;
He had no breath, no being, but in hers;

She was his voice; he did not speak to her,
But trembled on her words; she was his sight,
For his eye follow'd hers, and saw with hers,
Which colour'd all his objects: he had ceased
To live within himself; she was his life,
The ocean to the river of his thoughts,
Which terminated all: upon a tone,
A touch of hers, his blood would ebb and flow,
And his cheek change tempestuously—his heart
Unknowing of its cause of agony.
But she in these fond feelings had no share:
Her sighs were not for him; to her he was
Even as a brother—but no more; 't was much,
For brotherless she was, save in the name
Her infant friendship had bestowed on him;
Herself the solitary scion left
Of a time-honour'd race.—It was a name
Which pleased him, and yet pleased him not—and why?
Time taught him a deep answer—when she loved
Another; even now she loved another,
And on the summit of that hill she stood
Looking afar if yet her lover's steed
Kept pace with her expectancy, and flew.

### III

A change came o'er the spirit of my dream.
There was an ancient mansion, and before
Its walls there was a steed caparison'd:
Within an antique Oratory stood
The Boy of whom I spake;—he was alone,
And pale, and pacing to and fro: anon

He sate him down, and seized a pen, and traced
Words which I could not guess of; then he lean'd
His bow'd head on his hands, and shook as 't were
With a convulsion—then arose again,
And with his teeth and quivering hands did tear
What he had written, but he shed no tears,
And he did calm himself, and fix his brow
Into a kind of quiet: as he paused,
The Lady of his love re-entered there;
She was serene and smiling then, and yet
She knew she was by him beloved,—she knew,
For quickly comes such knowledge, that his heart
Was darken'd with her shadow, and she saw
That he was wretched, but she saw not all.
He rose, and with a cold and gentle grasp
He took her hand; a moment o'er his face
A tablet of unutterable thoughts
Was traced, and then it faded, as it came;
He dropp'd the hand he held, and with slow steps
Retired, but not as bidding her adieu,
For they did part with mutual smiles; he pass'd
From out the massy gate of that old Hall,
And mounting on his steed he went his way;
And ne'er repass'd that hoary threshold more.

## IV

A change came o'er the spirit of my dream.
The Boy was sprung to manhood: in the wilds
Of fiery climes he made himself a home,
And his soul drank their sunbeams: he was girt
With strange and dusky aspects; he was not

Himself like what he had been; on the sea
And on the shore he was a wanderer;
There was a mass of many images
Crowded like waves upon me, but he was
A part of all; and in the last he lay
Reposing from the noontide sultriness,
Couch'd among fallen columns, in the shade
Of ruin'd walls that had survived the names
Of those who rear'd them; by his sleeping side
Stood camels grazing, and some goodly steeds
Were fasten'd near a fountain; and a man
Clad in a flowing garb did watch the while,
While many of his tribe slumber'd around:
And they were canopied by the blue sky,
So cloudless, clear, and purely beautiful,
That God alone was to be seen in heaven.

## V

A change came o'er the spirit of my dream.
The Lady of his love was wed with One
Who did not love her better:—in her home,
A thousand leagues from his,—her native home,
She dwelt, begirt with growing Infancy,
Daughters and sons of Beauty,—but behold!
Upon her face there was the tint of grief,
The settled shadow of an inward strife,
And an unquiet drooping of the eye,
As if its lid were charged with unshed tears.
What could her grief be?—she had all she loved,
And he who had so loved her was not there
To trouble with bad hopes, or evil wish,

Or ill-repress'd affliction, her pure thoughts.
What could her grief be?—she had loved him not,
Nor given him cause to deem himself beloved,
Nor could he be a part of that which prey'd
Upon her mind—a spectre of the past.


## VI


A change came o'er the spirit of my dream.
The Wanderer was return'd.—I saw him stand
Before an Altar—with a gentle bride;
Her face was fair, but was not that which made
The Starlight of his Boyhood;—as he stood
Even at the Altar, o'er his brow there came
The self-same aspect, and the quivering shock
That in the antique Oratory shook
His bosom in its solitude; and then—
As in that hour—a moment o'er his face
The tablet of unutterable thoughts
Was traced,—and then it faded as it came,
And he stood calm and quiet, and he spoke
The fitting vows, but heard not his own words,
And all things reel'd around him; he could see
Not that which was, nor that which should have been
But the old mansions, and the accustom'd hall,
And the remember'd chambers, and the place,
The day, the hour, the sunshine, and the shade,
All things pertaining to that place and hour,
And her who was his destiny,—came back
And thrust themselves between him and the light:
What business had they there at such a time?

## VII

A change came o'er the spirit of my dream.
The Lady of his love;—Oh! she was changed
As by the sickness of the soul; her mind
Had wander'd from its dwelling, and her eyes
They had not their own lustre, but the look
Which is not of the earth; she was become
The queen of a fantastic realm; her thoughts
Were combinations of disjointed things;
And forms impalpable and unperceived
Of others' sight familiar were to hers.
And this the world calls frenzy; but the wise
Have a far deeper madness, and the glance
Of melancholy is a fearful gift;
What is it but the telescope of truth?
Which strips the distance of its fantasies,
And brings life near in utter nakedness,
Making the cold reality too real!

## VIII

A change came o'er the spirit of my dream.
The Wanderer was alone as heretofore,
The beings which surrounded him were gone,
Or were at war with him; he was a mark
For blight and desolation, compass'd round
With Hatred and Contention; Pain was mix'd
In all which was served up to him, until,
Like to the Pontic monarch of old days,
He fed on poisons, and they had no power,
But were a kind of nutriment; he lived

Through that which had been death to many men,
And made him friends of mountains: with the stars
And the quick Spirit of the Universe
He held his dialogues; and they did teach
To him the magic of their mysteries;
To him the book of Night was open'd wide,
And voices from the deep abyss reveal'd
A marvel and a secret—Be it so.

## IX

My dream was past; it had no further change.
It was of a strange order, that the doom
Of these two creatures should be thus traced out
Almost like a reality—the one
To end in madness—both in misery.

# GEORGE GORDON BYRON

*[*From]* *Childe Harold's Pilgrimage*

[*From*] Canto the Third

### I

Is thy face like thy mother's, my fair child!
Ada! sole daughter of my house and heart?
When last I saw thy young blue eyes they smiled,
And then we parted,—not as now we part,
But with a hope.—
                    Awaking with a start,
The waters heave around me; and on high
The winds lift up their voices: I depart,
Whither I know not; but the hour's gone by,
When Albion's lessening shores should grieve or glad mine **eye.**

### II

Once more upon the waters! yet once more!
And the waves bound beneath me as a steed
That knows his rider. Welcome to their roar!
Swift by their guidance, wheresoe'er it lead!
Though the strain'd mast should quiver as a reed,
And the rent canvas fluttering strew the gale,
Still must I on; for I am as a weed,
Flung from the rock, on Ocean's foam to sail
Where'er the surge may sweep, the tempest's breath **prevail.**

### III

In my youth's summer I did sing of One,
The wandering outlaw of his own dark mind;
Again I seize the theme, then but begun,
And bear it with me, as the rushing wind
Bears the cloud onwards: in the Tale I find
The furrows of long thought, and dried-up tears,
Which, ebbing, leave a sterile track behind,
O'er which all heavily the journeying years
Plod the last sands of life,—where not a flower appears.

### IV

Since my young days of passion—joy, or pain,
Perchance my heart and harp have lost a string,
And both may jar: it may be, that in vain
I would essay as I have sung to sing.
Yet, though a dreary strain, to this I cling;
So that it wean me from the weary dream
Of selfish grief or gladness—so it fling
Forgetfulness around me—it shall seem
To me, though no one else, a not ungrateful theme.

### V

He, who grown aged in this world of woe,
In deeds, not years, piercing the depths of life,
So that no wonder waits him; nor below
Can love or sorrow, fame, ambition, strife,
Cut to his heart again with the keen knife
Of silent, sharp endurance: he can tell
Why thought seeks refuge in lone caves, yet rife
With airy images, and shapes which dwell
Still unimpair'd, though old, in the soul's haunted cell.

## VI

'Tis to create, and in creating live
A being more intense that we endow
With form our fancy, gaining as we give
The life we image, even as I do now.
What am I? Nothing: but not so art thou,
Soul of my thought! with whom I traverse earth,
Invisible but gazing, as I glow
Mix'd with thy spirit, blended with thy birth,
And feeling still with thee in my crush'd feelings' dearth.

## VII

Yet must I think less wildly:—I *have* thought
Too long and darkly, till my brain became,
In its own eddy boiling and o'erwrought,
A whirling gulf of fantasy and flame:
And thus, untaught in youth my heart to tame,
My springs of life were poison'd. 'Tis too late!
Yet I am changed; though still enough the same
In strength to bear what time cannot abate,
And feed on bitter fruits without accusing Fate.

## VIII

Something too much of this:—but now 'tis past,
And the spell closes with its silent seal.
Long absent HAROLD re-appears at last;
He of the breast which fain no more would feel,
Wrung with the wounds which kill not, but ne'er heal;
Yet Time, who changes all, had alter'd him
In soul and aspect as in age: years steal
Fire from the mind as vigour from the limb;
And life's enchanted cup but sparkles near the brim.

### IX

His had been quaff'd too quickly, and he found
The dregs were wormwood; but he fill'd again,
And from a purer fount, on holier ground,
And deem'd its spring perpetual; but in vain!
Still round him clung invisibly a chain
Which gall'd for ever, fettering though unseen,
And heavy though it clank'd not; worn with pain,
Which pined although it spoke not, and grew keen,
Entering with every step he took through many a scene.

### X

Secure in guarded coldness, he had mix'd
Again in fancied safety with his kind,
And deem'd his spirit now so firmly fix'd
And sheath'd with an unvulnerable mind,
That, if no joy, no sorrow lurk'd behind;
And he, as one, might 'midst the many stand
Unheeded, searching through the crowd to find
Fit speculation; such as in strange land
He found in wonder-works of God and Nature's hand.

### XI

But who can view the ripen'd rose, nor seek
To wear it? who can curiously behold
The smoothness and the sheen of beauty's cheek,
Nor feel the heart can never all grow old?
Who can contemplate Fame through clouds unfold
The star which rises o'er her steep, nor climb?
Harold, once more within the vortex, roll'd
On with the giddy circle, chasing Time,
Yet with a nobler aim than in his youth's fond prime.

## XII

But soon he knew himself the most unfit
Of men to herd with Man; with whom he held
Little in common; untaught to submit
His thoughts to others, though his soul was quell'd
In youth by his own thoughts; still uncompell'd,
He would not yield dominion of his mind
To spirits against whom his own rebell'd;
Proud though in desolation; which could find
life within itself, to breathe without mankind.

## XIII

Where rose the mountains, there to him were friends;
Where roll'd the ocean, thereon was his home;
Where a blue sky, and glowing clime, extends,
He had the passion and the power to roam;
The desert, forest, cavern, breaker's foam,
Were unto him companionship; they spake
A mutual language, clearer than the tome
Of his land's tongue, which he would oft forsake
or Nature's pages glass'd by sunbeams on the lake.

## XIV

Like the Chaldean, he could watch the stars,
Till he had peopled them with beings bright
As their own beams; and earth, and earth-born jars,
And human frailties, were forgotten quite:
Could he have kept his spirit to that flight
He had been happy; but this clay will sink
Its spark immortal, envying it the light
To which it mounts, as if to break the link
at keeps us from yon heaven which woos us to its brink.

## XV

But in Man's dwellings he became a thing
Restless and worn, and stern and wearisome,
Droop'd as a wild-born falcon with clipt wing,
To whom the boundless air alone were home:
Then came his fit again, which to o'ercome,
As eagerly the barr'd-up bird will beat
His breast and beak against his wiry dome
Till the blood tinge his plumage, so the heat
Of his impeded soul would through his bosom eat.

# GEORGE GORDON BYRON

[From] *Don Juan*

[*From*] Canto the Second

### LXX

The fourth day came, but not a breath of air,
  And Ocean slumbered like an unweaned child:
The fifth day, and their boat lay floating there,
  The sea and sky were blue, and clear, and mild—
With their own oar (I wish they had had a pair)
  What could they do? and Hunger's rage grew wild:
So Juan's spaniel, spite of his entreating,
Was killed, and portioned out for present eating.

### LXXI

On the sixth day they fed upon his hide,
  And Juan, who had still refused, because
The creature was his father's dog that died,
  Now feeling all the vulture in his jaws,
With some remorse received (though first denied)
  As a great favour one of the fore-paws,
Which he divided with Pedrillo, who
Devoured it, longing for the other too.

## LXXII

The seventh day, and no wind—the burning sun
   Blistered and scorched, and stagnant on the sea,
They lay like carcasses; and hope was none,
   Save in the breeze that came not: savagely
They glared upon each other—all was done,
   Water, and wine, and food,—and you might see
The longings of the cannibals arise
(Although they spoke not) in their wolfish eyes.
   'T was but his own, suppressed till now, he found:
And out they spoke of lots for flesh and blood,
And who should die to be his fellow's food.


## LXXIII

At length one whispered his companion, who
   Whispered another, and thus it went round,
And then into a hoarser murmur grew,
   An ominous, and wild, and desperate sound;
And when his comrade's thought each sufferer knew,
   'T was but his own, suppressed till now, he found:
And out they spoke of lots for flesh and blood,
And who should die to be his fellow's food.


## LXXIV

But ere they came to this, they that day shared
   Some leathern caps, and what remained of shoes;
And then they looked around them, and despaired,
   And none to be the sacrifice would choose;

At length the lots were torn up, and prepared,
　　But of materials that must shock the Muse—
Having no paper, for the want of better,
They took by force from Juan, Julia's letter.


## LXXV

The lots were made, and marked, and mixed, and handed,
　　In silent horror, and their distribution
Lulled even the savage hunger which demanded,
　　Like the Promethean vulture, this pollution;
None in particular had sought or planned it,
　　'T was Nature gnawed them to this resolution,
By which none were permitted to be neuter—
And the lot fell on Juan's luckless tutor.


## LXXVI

He but requested to be bled to death:
　　The surgeon had his instruments, and bled
Pedrillo, and so gently ebbed his breath,
　　You hardly could perceive when he was dead.
He died as born, a Catholic in faith,
　　Like most in the belief in which they're bred,
And first a little crucifix he kissed,
And then held out his jugular and wrist.


## LXXVII

The surgeon, as there was no other fee,
　　Had his first choice of morsels for his pains;
But being thirstiest at the moment, he
　　Preferred a draught from the fast-flowing veins:

Part was divided, part thrown in the sea,
    And such things as the entrails and the brains
Regaled two sharks, who followed o'er the billow—
    The sailors ate the rest of poor Pedrillo.

### LXXVIII

The sailors ate him, all save three, or four,
    Who were not quite so fond of animal food;
To these was added Juan, who, before
    Refusing his own spaniel, hardly could
Feel now his appetite increased much more;
    'T was not to be expected that he should,
Even in extremity of their disaster,
Dine with them on his pastor and his master.

### LXXIX

'T was better that he did not; for, in fact,
    The consequence was awful in the extreme;
For they, who were most ravenous in the act,
    Went raging mad—Lord! how they did blaspheme!
And foam, and roll, with strange convulsions racked,
    Drinking salt-water like a mountain-stream,
Tearing, and grinning, howling, screeching, swearing,
And, with hyæna-laughter, died despairing.

### LXXX

Their number were much thinned by this infliction,
    And all the rest were thin enough, Heaven knows;
And some of them had lost their recollection,
    Happier than they who still perceived their woes;

But others pondered on a new dissection,
    As if not warned sufficiently by those
Who had already perished, suffering madly,
For having used their appetites so sadly.

## LXXXI

And next they thought upon the master's mate,
    As fattest; but he saved himself, because,
Besides being much averse from such a fate,
    There were some other reasons: the first was,
He had been rather indisposed of late;
    And—that which chiefly proved his saving clause—
Was a small present made to him at Cadiz,
By general subscription of the ladies.

## LXXXII

Of poor Pedrillo something still remained,
    But was used sparingly,—some were afraid,
And others still their appetites constrained,
    Or but at times a little supper made;
All except Juan, who throughout abstained,
    Chewing a piece of bamboo, and some lead:
At length they caught two Boobies, and a Noddy,
And then they left of eating the dead body.

## LXXXIII

And if Pedrillo's fate should shocking be,
    Remember Ugolino condescends
To eat the head of his arch-enemy
    The moment after he politely ends

His tale: if foes be food in Hell, at sea
   'T is surely fair to dine upon our friends,
When Shipwreck's short allowance grows too scanty,
Without being much more horrible than Dante.

### LXXXIV

And the same night there fell a shower of rain,
   For which their mouths gaped, like the cracks of ear
When dried to summer dust; till taught by pain,
   Men really know not what good water's worth;
If you had been in Turkey or in Spain,
   Or with a famished boat's crew had your berth,
Or in the desert heard the camel's bell,
You'd wish yourself where Truth is—in a well.

### LXXXV

It poured down torrents, but they were no richer
   Until they found a ragged piece of sheet,
Which served them as a sort of spongy pitcher,
   And when they deemed its moisture was complete,
They wrung it out, and though a thirsty ditcher
   Might not have thought the scanty draught so sweet
As a full pot of porter, to their thinking
They ne'er till now had known the joys of drinking.

### LXXXVI

And their baked lips, with many a bloody crack,
   Sucked in the moisture, which like nectar streamed;
Their throats were ovens, their swoln tongues were bla⟨
   As the rich man's in Hell, who vainly screamed

To beg the beggar, who could not rain back
    A drop of dew, when every drop had seemed
To taste of Heaven—If this be true, indeed,
Some Christians have a comfortable creed.

## LXXXVII

There were two fathers in this ghastly crew,
    And with them their two sons, of whom the one
Was more robust and hardy to the view,
    But he died early; and when he was gone,
His nearest messmate told his sire, who threw
    One glance at him, and said, "Heaven's will be done!
I can do nothing," and he saw him thrown
Into the deep without a tear or groan.

## LXXXVIII

The other father had a weaklier child,
    Of a soft cheek, and aspect delicate;
But the boy bore up long, and with a mild
    And patient spirit held aloof his fate;
Little he said, and now and then he smiled,
    As if to win a part from off the weight
He saw increasing on his father's heart,
With the deep deadly thought, that they must part.

## LXXXIX

And o'er him bent his sire, and never raised
    His eyes from off his face, but wiped the foam
From his pale lips, and ever on him gazed,
    And when the wished-for shower at length was come,

[193

And the boy's eyes, which the dull film half glazed,
  Brightened, and for a moment seemed to roam,
He squeezed from out a rag some drops of rain
Into his dying child's mouth—but in vain.

## XC

The boy expired—the father held the clay,
  And looked upon it long, and when at last
Death left no doubt, and the dead burthen lay
  Stiff on his heart, and pulse and hope were past,
He watched it wistfully, until away
  'T was borne by the rude wave wherein 't was cast;
Then he himself sank down all dumb and shivering,
And gave no sign of life, save his limbs quivering.

## XCI

Now overhead a rainbow, bursting through
  The scattering clouds, shone, spanning the dark sea,
Resting its bright base on the quivering blue;
  And all within its arch appeared to be
Clearer than that without, and its wide hue
  Waxed broad and waving, like a banner free,
Then changed like to a bow that's bent, and then
Forsook the dim eyes of these shipwrecked men.

## XCII

It changed, of course; a heavenly Chameleon,
  The airy child of vapour and the sun,
Brought forth in purple, cradled in vermilion,
  Baptized in molten gold, and swathed in dun,

# GEORGE GORDON BYRON

Glittering like crescents o'er a Turk's pavilion,
  And blending every colour into one,
Just like a black eye in a recent scuffle
(For sometimes we must box without the muffle).

## XCIII

Our shipwrecked seamen thought it a good omen—
  It is as well to think so, now and then;
'T was an old custom of the Greek and Roman,
  And may become of great advantage when
Folks are discouraged; and most surely no men
  Had greater need to nerve themselves again
Than these, and so this rainbow looked like Hope—
Quite a celestial Kaleidoscope.

## XCIV

About this time a beautiful white bird,
  Webfooted, not unlike a dove in size
And plumage (probably it might have erred
  Upon its course), passed oft before their eyes,
And tried to perch, although it saw and heard
  The men within the boat, and in this guise
It came and went, and fluttered round them till
Night fell:—this seemed a better omen still.

## XCV

But in this case I also must remark,
  'T was well this bird of promise did not perch,
Because the tackle of our shattered bark
  Was not so safe for roosting as a church;

And had it been the dove from Noah's ark,
   Returning there from her successful search,
Which in their way that moment chanced to fall,
They would have eat her, olive-branch and all.

## XCVI

With twilight it again came on to blow,
   But not with violence; the stars shone out,
The boat made way; yet now they were so low,
   They knew not where nor what they were about;
Some fancied they saw land, and some said "No!"
   The frequent fog-banks gave them cause to doubt—
Some swore that they heard breakers, others guns,
And all mistook about the latter once.

## XCVII

As morning broke, the light wind died away,
   When he who had the watch sung out and swore,
If 't was not land that rose with the Sun's ray,
   He wished that land he never might see more;
And the rest rubbed their eyes and saw a bay,
   Or thought they saw, and shaped their course for shore
For shore it was, and gradually grew
Distinct, and high, and palpable to view.

## XCVIII

And then of these some part burst into tears,
   And others, looking with a stupid stare,
Could not yet separate their hopes from fears,
   And seemed as if they had no further care;

While a few prayed—(the first time for some years)—
  And at the bottom of the boat three were
Asleep: they shook them by the hand and head,
And tried to awaken them, but found them dead.


XCIX

The day before, fast sleeping on the water,
  They found a turtle of the hawk's-bill kind,
And by good fortune, gliding softly, caught her,
  Which yielded a day's life, and to their mind
Proved even still a more nutritious matter,
  Because it left encouragement behind:
They thought that in such perils, more than chance
Had sent them this for their deliverance.


C

The land appeared a high and rocky coast,
  And higher grew the mountains as they drew,
Set by a current, toward it: they were lost
  In various conjectures, for none knew
To what part of the earth they had been tost,
  So changeable had been the winds that blew;
Some thought it was Mount Aetna, some the highlands
Of Candia, Cyprus, Rhodes, or other islands.


CI

Meantime the current, with a rising gale,
  Still set them onwards to the welcome shore,
Like Charon's bark of spectres, dull and pale:
  Their living freight was now reduced to four,

[197

And three dead, whom their strength could not avail
   To heave into the deep with those before,
Though the two sharks still followed them, and dashed
The spray into their faces as they splashed.

### CII

Famine—despair—cold—thirst and heat, had done
   Their work on them by turns, and thinned them to
Such things a mother had not known her son
   Amidst the skeletons of that gaunt crew;
By night chilled, by day scorched, thus one by one
   They perished, until withered to these few,
But chiefly by a species of self-slaughter,
In washing down Pedrillo with salt water.

### CIII

As they drew nigh the land, which now was seen
   Unequal in its aspect here and there,
They felt the freshness of its growing green,
   That waved in forest-tops, and smoothed the air,
And fell upon their glazed eyes like a screen
   From glistening waves, and skies so hot and bare—
Lovely seemed any object that should sweep
Away the vast—salt—dread—eternal Deep.

### CIV

The shore looked wild, without a trace of man,
   And girt by formidable waves; but they
Were made for land, and thus their course they ran,
   Though right ahead the roaring breakers lay:

A reef between them also now began
  To show its boiling surf and bounding spray,
But finding no place for their landing better,
They ran the boat for shore,—and overset her.

.    .    .    .    .    .    .    .    .

## CLXXXV

They looked up to the sky, whose floating glow
  Spread like a rosy Ocean, vast and bright;
They gazed upon the glittering sea below,
  Whence the broad Moon rose circling into sight;
They heard the waves' splash, and the wind so low,
  And saw each other's dark eyes darting light
Into each other—and, beholding this,
Their lips drew near, and clung into a kiss;

## CLXXXVI

A long, long kiss, a kiss of Youth and Love,
  And Beauty, all concentrating like rays
Into one focus, kindled from above;
  Such kisses as belong to early days,
Where Heart, and Soul, and Sense, in concert move,
  And the blood's lava, and the pulse of blaze,
Each kiss a heart-quake,—for a kiss's strength,
I think, it must be reckoned by its length.

## CLXXXVII

By length I mean duration; theirs endured
  Heaven knows how long—no doubt they never reck-
    oned;
And if they had, they could not have secured
  The sum of their sensations to a second:

# GEORGE GORDON BYRON

They had not spoken, but they felt allured,
　As if their souls and lips each other beckoned,
Which, being joined, like swarming bees they clung—
Their hearts the flowers from whence the honey sprung

## CLXXXVIII

They were alone, but not alone as they
　Who shut in chambers think it loneliness;
The silent Ocean, and the starlight bay,
　The twilight glow, which momently grew less,
The voiceless sands, and dropping caves, that lay
　Around them, made them to each other press,
As if there were no life beneath the sky
Save theirs, and that their life could never die.

## CLXXXIX

They feared no eyes nor ears on that lone beach;
　They felt no terrors from the night; they were
All in all to each other: though their speech
　Was broken words, they *thought* a language there,—
And all the burning tongues the Passions teach
　Found in one sigh the best interpreter
Of Nature's oracle—first love—that all
Which Eve has left her daughters since her fall.

## CXC

Haidèe spoke not of scruples, asked no vows,
　Nor offered any; she had never heard
Of plight and promises to be a spouse,
　Or perils by a loving maid incurred;

She was all which pure Ignorance allows,
    And flew to her young mate like a young bird;
And, never having dreamt of falsehood, she
Had not one word to say of constancy.

## CXCI

She loved, and was beloved—she adored,
    And she was worshipped after Nature's fashion—
Their intense souls, into each other poured,
    If souls could die, had perished in that passion,—
But by degrees their senses were restored,
    Again to be o'ercome, again to dash on;
And, beating 'gainst *his* bosom, Haidèe's heart
Felt as if never more to beat apart.

## CXCII

Alas! they were so young, so beautiful,
    So lonely, loving, helpless, and the hour
Was that in which the Heart is always full,
    And, having o'er itself no further power,
Prompts deeds Eternity can not annul,
    But pays off moments in an endless shower
Of hell-fire—all prepared for people giving
Pleasure or pain to one another living.

## CXCIII

Alas! for Juan and Haidèe! they were
    So loving and so lovely—till then never,
Excepting our first parents, such a pair
    Had run the risk of being damned for ever:

And Haidèe, being devout as well as fair,
  Had, doubtless, heard about the Stygian river,
And Hell and Purgatory—but forgot
Just in the very crisis she should not.

## CXCIV

They look upon each other, and their eyes
  Gleam in the moonlight; and her white arm clasps
Round Juan's head, and his around her lies
  Half buried in the tresses which it grasps;
She sits upon his knee, and drinks his sighs,
  He hers, until they end in broken gasps;
And thus they form a group that's quite antique,
Half naked, loving, natural, and Greek.

## CXCV

And when those deep and burning moments passed,
  And Juan sunk to sleep within her arms,
She slept not, but all tenderly, though fast,
  Sustained his head upon her bosom's charms
And now and then her eye to Heaven is cast,
  And then on the pale cheek her breast now warms,
Pillowed on her o'erflowing heart, which pants
With all it granted, and with all it grants.

## CXCVI

An infant when it gazes on a light,
  A child the moment when it drains the breast,
A devote when she soars the Host in sight,
  An Arab with a stranger for a guest,

## GEORGE GORDON BYRON

A sailor when the prize has struck in fight,
    A miser filling his most hoarded chest,
Feel rapture; but not such true joy are reaping
As they who watch o'er what they love while sleeping.

### CXCVII

For there it lies so tranquil, so beloved,
    All that it hath of Life with us is living;
So gentle, stirless, helpless, and unmoved,
    And all unconscious of the joy 't is giving;
All it hath felt, inflicted, passed, and proved,
    Hushed into depths beyond the watcher's diving:
There lies the thing we love with all its errors
And all its charms, like Death without its terrors.

### CXCVIII

The Lady watched her lover—and that hour
    Of Love's, and Night's, and Ocean's solitude
O'erflowed her soul with their united power;
    Amidst the barren sand and rocks so rude
She and her wave-worn love had made their bower,
    Where nought upon their passion could intrude,
And all the stars that crowded the blue space
Saw nothing happier than her glowing face.

# PERCY BYSSHE SHELLEY

*Stanzas—April, 1814*

Away! the moor is dark beneath the moon,
Rapid clouds have drunk the last pale beam of even:
Away! the gathering winds will call the darkness soon
And profoundest midnight shroud the serene lights of
heaven.
Pause not! the time is past! Every voice cries 'Away!'
Tempt not with one last tear thy friend's ungentle mood:
Thy lover's eye, so glazed and cold, dares not entreat thy stay:
Duty and dereliction guide thee back to solitude.

Away, away! to thy sad and silent home;
Pour bitter tears on its desolated hearth;
Watch the dim shades as like ghosts they go and come
And complicate strange webs of melancholy mirth
The leaves of wasted autumn woods shall float around thine head
The blooms of dewy Spring shall gleam beneath thy feet
But thy soul or this world must fade in the frost that bind
the dead,
Ere midnight's frown and morning's smile, ere thou and peace
may meet.

The cloud-shadows of Midnight possess their own repose
For the weary winds are silent, or the moon is in the deep;

Some respite to its turbulence unresting ocean knows:
Whatever moves or toils or grieves hath its appointed sleep.

Thou in the grave shall rest:—yet, till the phantoms flee
Which that house and heath and garden made dear to thee
    erewhile,
Thy remembrance and repentance and deep musings are not free
From the music of two voices, and the light of one sweet smile.

# PERCY BYSSHE SHELLEY

*Stanzas Written in Dejection Near Naples*

### I

The sun is warm, the sky is clear,
    The waves are dancing fast and bright,
Blue isles and snowy mountains wear
    The purple noon's transparent might;
    The breath of the moist earth is light
Around its unexpanded buds;
    Like many a voice of one delight,
    The wind's, the bird's, the ocean-floods',
The city's voice itself is soft like Solitude's.

### II

I see the deep's untrampled floor
    With green and purple sea-weeds strown;
I see the waves upon the shore,
    Like light dissolved in star-showers, thrown.
    I sit upon the sands alone.
The lightning of the noontide ocean
    Is flashing round me, and a tone
Arises from its measured motion,—
How sweet, did any heart now share in my emotion!

### III

Alas! I have nor hope nor health,
    Nor peace within nor calm around;
Nor that content, surpassing wealth,
    The sage in meditation found,
    And walked with inward glory crowned;
Nor fame nor power nor love nor leisure.
    Others I see whom these surround—
Smiling they live, and call life pleasure;—
To me that cup has been dealt in another measure.

### IV

Yet now despair itself is mild,
    Even as the winds and waters are;
I could lie down like a tired child,
    And weep away the life of care
    Which I have borne and yet must bear,—
Till death like sleep might steal on me,
    And I might feel in the warm air
My cheek grow cold, and hear the sea
Breathe o'er my dying brain its last monotony.

### V

Some might lament that I were cold,
    As I when this sweet day is gone,
Which my lost heart, too soon grown old,
    Insults with this untimely moan.
    They might lament—for I am one
Whom men love not, and yet regret;
    Unlike this day, which, when the sun
Shall on its stainless glory set,
Will linger, though enjoyed, like joy in memory yet.

# PERCY BYSSHE SHELLEY

## The Cloud

### I

I bring fresh showers for the thirsting flowers
    From the seas and the streams;
I bear light shade for the leaves when laid
    In their noonday dreams.
From my wings are shaken the dews that waken
    The sweet buds every one,
When rocked to rest on their Mother's breast,
    As she dances about the sun.
I wield the flail of the lashing hail,
    And whiten the green plains under;
And then again I dissolve it in rain,
    And laugh as I pass in thunder.

### II

I sift the snow on the mountains below,
    And their great pines groan aghast;
And all the night 'tis my pillow white,
    While I sleep in the arms of the Blast.
Sublime on the towers of my skiey bowers,
    Lightning my pilot sits;
In a cavern under is fettered the Thunder,
    It struggles and howls at fits.
Over earth and ocean with gentle motion
    This pilot is guiding me,

Lured by the love of the Genii that move
   In the depths of the purple sea;
Over the rills and the crags and the hills,
   Over the lakes and the plains,
Wherever he dream under mountain or stream
   The Spirit he loves remains;
And I all the while bask in heaven's blue smile,
   Whilst he is dissolving in rains.

### III

The sanguine Sunrise, with his meteor eyes,
   And his burning plumes outspread,
Leaps on the back of my sailing rack,
   When the morning star shines dead:
As on the jag of a mountain-crag
   Which an earthquake rocks and swings,
An eagle alit one moment may sit
   In the light of its golden wings.
And, when Sunset may breathe, from the lit sea beneath,
   Its ardours of rest and of love,
And the crimson pall of eve may fall
   From the depth of heaven above,
With wings folded I rest, on mine airy nest,
   As still as a brooding dove.

### IV

That orbèd maiden with white fire laden
   Whom mortals call the Moon
Glides glimmering o'er my fleece-like floor
   By the midnight breezes strewn;

PERCY BYSSHE SHELLEY

And wherever the beat of her unseen feet,
  Which only the angels hear,
May have broken the woof of my tent's thin roof,
  The Stars peep behind her and peer.
And I laugh to see them whirl and flee
  Like a swarm of golden bees
When I widen the rent in my wind-built tent,—
  Till the calm rivers, lakes, and seas,
Like strips of the sky fallen through me on high
  Are each paved with the moon and these.


V

I bind the Sun's throne with a burning zone,
  And the Moon's with a girdle of pearl;
The volcanoes are dim, and the Stars reel and swim,
  When the Whirlwinds my banner unfurl.
From cape to cape, with a bridge-like shape,
  Over a torrent sea,
Sunbeam-proof, I hang like a roof;
  The mountains its columns be.
The triumphal arch through which I march,
  With hurricane, fire, and snow,
When the Powers of the air are chained to my chair,
  Is the million-coloured bow;
The Sphere-fire above its soft colours wove,
  While the moist Earth was laughing below.


VI

I am the daughter of Earth and Water,
  And the nursling of the Sky:

I pass through the pores of the ocean and shores;
  I change but I cannot die.
For after the rain, when with never a stain
  The pavilion of heaven is bare,
And the winds and sunbeams with their convex gleams
  Build up the blue dome of air,
I silently laugh at my own cenotaph,—
  And out of the caverns of rain,
Like a child from the womb, like a ghost from the tomb,
  I arise and unbuild it again.

# PERCY BYSSHE SHELLEY

*Adonais: An Elegy on the Death of John Keats*

### I

I weep for Adonais—he is dead!
　　Oh weep for Adonais, though our tears
Thaw not the frost which binds so dear a head!
　　And thou, sad Hour selected from all years
　　To mourn our loss, rouse thy obscure compeers,
And teach them thine own sorrow! Say: 'With me
　　Died Adonais! Till the future dares
Forget the past, his fate and fame shall be
An echo and a light unto eternity.'

### II

Where wert thou, mighty Mother, when he lay,
　　When thy son lay, pierced by the shaft which flies
In darkness? Where was lorn Urania
　　When Adonais died? With veilèd eyes,
　　Mid listening Echoes, in her paradise
She sate, while one, with soft enamoured breath,
　　Rekindled all the fading melodies
With which, like flowers that mock the corse beneath,
He had adorned and hid the coming bulk of Death.

### III

Oh weep for Adonais—he is dead!—
  Wake, melancholy Mother, wake and weep!—
Yet wherefore? Quench within their burning bed
  Thy fiery tears, and let thy loud heart keep,
  Like his, a mute and uncomplaining sleep;
For he is gone where all things wise and fair
  Descend. Oh dream not that the amorous deep
Will yet restore him to the vital air;
Death feeds on his mute voice, and laughs at our despair.

### IV

Most musical of mourners, weep again!
  Lament anew, Urania!—He died
Who was the sire of an immortal strain,
  Blind, old, and lonely, when his country's pride
  The priest, the slave, and the liberticide,
Trampled and mocked with many a loathèd rite
  Of lust and blood. He went unterrified
Into the gulf of death; but his clear sprite
Yet reigns o'er earth, the third among the Sons of Light.

### V

Most musical of mourners, weep anew!
  Not all to that bright station dared to climb:
And happier they their happiness who knew,
  Whose tapers yet burn through that night of time
  In which suns perished. Others more sublime,
Struck by the envious wrath of man or god,
  Have sunk, extinct in their refulgent prime;
And some yet live, treading the thorny road
Which leads, through toil and hate, to Fame's serene abode.

PERCY BYSSHE SHELLEY

### VI

But now thy youngest, dearest one has perished,
    The nursling of thy widowhood, who grew,
Like a pale flower by some sad maiden cherished,
    And fed with true-love tears instead of dew.
    Most musical of mourners, weep anew!
Thy extreme hope, the loveliest and the last,
    The bloom whose petals, nipped before they blew,
Died on the promise of the fruit, is waste;
The broken lily lies—the storm is overpast.

### VII

To that high Capital where kingly Death
    Keeps his pale court in beauty and decay
He came; and bought, with price of purest breath,
    A grave among the eternal.—Come away!
    Haste, while the vault of blue Italian day
Is yet his fitting charnel-roof, while still
    He lies as if in dewy sleep he lay.
Awake him not! surely he takes his fill
Of deep and liquid rest, forgetful of all ill.

### VIII

He will awake no more, oh never more!
    Within the twilight chamber spreads apace
The shadow of white Death, and at the door
    Invisible Corruption waits to trace
    His extreme way to her dim dwelling-place;
The eternal Hunger sits, but pity and awe
    Soothe her pale rage, nor dares she to deface
So fair a prey, till darkness and the law
Of change shall o'er his sleep the mortal curtain draw.

## IX

Oh weep for Adonais!—The quick Dreams,
    The passion-wingèd ministers of thought,
Who were his flocks, whom near the living streams
    Of his young spirit he fed, and whom he taught
    The love which was its music, wander not—
Wander no more from kindling brain to brain,
    But droop there whence they sprung; and mourn their
        lot
Round the cold heart where, after their sweet pain,
They ne'er will gather strength or find a home again.

## X

And one with trembling hands clasps his cold head,
    And fans him with her moonlight wings, and cries,
'Our love, our hope, our sorrow, is not dead!
    See, on the silken fringe of his faint eyes,
    Like dew upon a sleeping flower, there lies
A tear some dream has loosened from his brain.'
    Lost angel of a ruined paradise!
She knew not 'twas her own,—as with no stain
She faded, like a cloud which had outwept its rain.

## XI

One from a lucid urn of starry dew
    Washed her light limbs, as if embalming them;
Another clipped her profuse locks, and threw
    The wreath upon him, like an anadem
    Which frozen tears instead of pearls begem;

Another in her wilful grief would break
   Her bow and wingèd reeds, as if to stem
A greater loss with one which was more weak,—
And dull the barbèd fire against his frozen cheek.


## XII

Another Splendour on his mouth alit,
   That mouth whence it was wont to draw the breath
Which gave it strength to pierce the guarded wit,
   And pass into the panting heart beneath
   With lightning and with music: the damp death
Quenched its caress upon his icy lips;
   And, as a dying meteor stains a wreath
Of moonlight vapour which the cold night clips,
It flushed through his pale limbs, and passed to its eclipse.


## XIII

And others came. Desires and Adorations;
   Wingèd Persuasions, and veiled Destinies;
Splendours, and Glooms, and glimmering Incarnations
   Of Hopes and Fears, and twilight Fantasies;
   And Sorrow, with her family of Sighs;
And Pleasure, blind with tears, led by the gleam
   Of her own dying smile instead of eyes,—
Came in slow pomp;—the moving pomp might seem
Like pageantry of mist on an autumnal stream.


## XIV

All he had loved, and moulded into thought
   From shape and hue and odour and sweet sound,

Lamented Adonais. Morning sought
    Her eastern watch-tower, and her hair unbound,
    Wet with the tears which should adorn the ground,
Dimmed the aërial eyes that kindle day;
    Afar the melancholy Thunder moaned,
Pale Ocean in unquiet slumber lay,
And the wild Winds flew round, sobbing in their dismay.


## XV

Lost Echo sits amid the voiceless mountains,
    And feeds her grief with his rememberd lay,
And will no more reply to winds or fountains,
    Or amorous birds perched on the young green spray,
    Or herdsman's horn, or bell at closing day;
Since she can mimic not his lips, more dear
    Than those for whose disdain she pined away
Into a shadow of all sounds:—a drear
Murmur, between their songs, is all the woodmen hear.


## XVI

Grief made the young Spring wild, and she threw down
    Her kindling buds, as if she Autumn were,
Or they dead leaves; since her delight is flown,
    For whom should she have waked the sullen Year?
    To Phoebus was not Hyacinth so dear,
Not to himself Narcissus, as to both
    Thou, Adonais; wan they stand and sere
Amid the faint companions of their youth,
With dew all turned to tears,—odour, to sighing ruth.

## XVII

Thy spirit's sister, the lorn nightingale,
    Mourns not her mate with such melodious pain;
Not so the eagle, who like thee could scale
    Heaven, and could nourish in the sun's domain
    Her mighty youth with morning, doth complain,
Soaring and screaming round her empty nest,
    As Albion wails for thee: the curse of Cain
Light on his head who pierced thy innocent breast,
And scared the angel soul that was its earthly guest!

## XVIII

Ah woe is me! Winter is come and gone,
    But grief returns with the revolving year.
The airs and streams renew their joyous tone;
    The ants, the bees, the swallows, re-appear;
    Fresh leaves and flowers deck the dead Seasons' bier;
The amorous birds now pair in every brake,
    And build their mossy homes in field and brere;
And the green lizard and the golden snake,
Like unimprisoned flames, out of their trance awake.

## XIX

Through wood and stream and field and hill and ocean
    A quickening life from the Earth's heart has burst,
As it has ever done, with change and motion,
    From the great morning of the world when first
    God dawned on chaos. In its stream immersed,
The lamps of heaven flash with a softer light;
    All baser things pant with life's sacred thirst,
Diffuse themselves, and spend in love's delight
The beauty and the joy of their renewèd might.

## XX

The leprous corpse, touched by this spirit tender,
　　Exhales itself in flowers of gentle breath;
Like incarnations of the stars, when splendour
　　Is changed to fragrance, they illumine death,
　　And mock the merry worm that wakes beneath.
Nought we know dies: shall that alone which knows
　　Be as a sword consumed before the sheath
By sightless lightning? The intense atom glows
A moment, then is quenched in a most cold repose.

## XXI

Alas, that all we loved of him should be,
　　But for our grief, as if it had not been,
And grief itself be mortal! Woe is me!
　　Whence are we, and why are we? of what scene
　　The actors and spectators? Great and mean
Meet massed in death, who lends what life must borrow.
　　As long as skies are blue and fields are green,
Evening must usher night, night urge the morrow,
Month follow month with woe, and year wake year to sorrow.

## XXII

He will awake no more, oh never more!
　　'Wake thou,' cried Misery, 'childless Mother! Rise
Out of thy sleep, and slake in thy heart's core
　　A wound more fierce than his, with tears and sighs.'
　　And all the Dreams that watched Urania's eyes,
And all the Echoes whom their Sister's song
　　Had held in holy silence, cried 'Arise';
Swift as a thought by the snake Memory stung,
From her ambrosial rest the fading Splendour sprung.

## XXIII

She rose like an autumnal Night that springs
   Out of the east, and follows wild and drear
The golden Day, which, on eternal wings,
   Even as a ghost abandoning a bier,
   Had left the Earth a corpse. Sorrow and fear
So struck, so roused, so rapt, Urania;
   So saddened round her like an atmosphere
Of stormy mist; so swept her on her way,
Even to the mournful place where Adonais lay.

## XXIV

Out of her secret paradise she sped,
   Through camps and cities rough with stone and ste
And human hearts, which, to her aery tread
   Yielding not, wounded the invisible
   Palms of her tender feet where'er they fell.
And barbèd tongues, and thoughts more sharp than the
   Rent the soft form they never could repel,
Whose sacred blood, like the young tears of May,
Paved with eternal flowers that undeserving way.

## XXV

In the death-chamber for a moment Death,
   Shamed by the presence of that living Might,
Blushed to annihilation, and the breath
   Revisited those lips, and life's pale light
   Flashed through those limbs so late her dear deligh

'Leave me not wild and drear and comfortless,
   As silent lightning leaves the starless night!
Leave me not!' cried Urania. Her distress
Roused Death: Death rose and smiled, and met her vain
   caress.

## XXVI

'Stay yet awhile! speak to me once again!
   Kiss me, so long but as a kiss may live!
And in my heartless breast and burning brain
   That word, that kiss, shall all thoughts else survive,
   With food of saddest memory kept alive,
Now thou art dead, as if it were a part
   Of thee, my Adonais! I would give
All that I am, to be as thou now art:—
But I am chained to Time, and cannot thence depart.

## XXVII

'O gentle child, beautiful as thou wert,
   Why didst thou leave the trodden paths of men
Too soon, and with weak hands though mighty heart
   Dare the unpastured dragon in his den?
   Defenceless as thou wert, oh where was then
Wisdom the mirrored shield, or Scorn the spear?
   Or, hadst thou waited the full cycle when
Thy spirit should have filled its crescent sphere,
The monsters of life's waste had fled from thee like deer.

## XXVIII

'The herded wolves bold only to pursue,
   The obscene ravens clamorous o'er the dead,

The vultures to the conqueror's banner true,
  Who feed where Desolation first has fed,
  And whose wings rain contagion,—how they fled,
When, like Apollo from his golden bow,
  The Pythian of the age one arrow sped,
  And smiled! —The spoilers tempt no second blow,
They fawn on the proud feet that spurn them lying low.

### XXIX

'The sun comes forth, and many reptiles spawn;
  He sets, and each ephemeral insect then
Is gathered into death without a dawn,
  And the immortal stars awake again.
  So is it in the world of living men:
A godlike mind soars forth, in its delight
  Making earth bare and veiling heaven; and, when
It sinks, the swarms that dimmed or shared its light
Leave to its kindred lamps the spirit's awful night.'

### XXX*

Thus ceased she: and the Mountain Shepherds came,
  Their garlands sere, their magic mantles rent.
The Pilgrim of Eternity, whose fame
  Over his living head like heaven is bent,
  An early but enduring monument,
Came, veiling all the lightnings of his song
  In sorrow. From her wilds Ierne sent
The sweetest lyrist of her saddest wrong,
And love taught grief to fall like music from his tongue.

* The poets referred to in stanzas XXX-XXXV are Byron, Moore, Shelley himself, and Leigh Hunt.

## XXXI

Midst others of less note came one frail form,
    A phantom among men, companionless
As the last cloud of an expiring storm,
    Whose thunder is its knell. He, as I guess,
    Had gazed on Nature's naked loveliness
Actaeon-like; and now he fled astray
    With feeble steps o'er the world's wilderness,
And his own thoughts along that rugged way
Pursued like raging hounds their father and their prey.

## XXXII

A pard-like Spirit beautiful and swift—
    A love in desolation masked—a power
Girt round with weakness; it can scarce uplift
    The weight of the superincumbent hour.
    It is a dying lamp, a falling shower,
A breaking billow;—even whilst we speak
    Is it not broken? On the withering flower
The killing sun smiles brightly: on a cheek
The life can burn in blood even while the heart may break.

## XXXIII

His head was bound with pansies overblown,
    And faded violets, white and pied and blue;
And a light spear topped with a cypress-cone,
    Round whose rude shaft dark ivy-tresses grew
    Yet dripping with the forest's noonday dew,
Vibrated, as the ever-beating heart
    Shook the weak hand that grasped it. Of that crew
He came the last, neglected and apart;
A herd-abandoned deer struck by the hunter's dart.

## XXXIV

All stood aloof, and at his partial moan
    Smiled through their tears. Well knew that gentle band
Who in another's fate now wept his own.
    As in the accents of an unknown land
    He sang new sorrow, sad Urania scanned
The Stranger's mien, and murmured 'Who art thou?'
    He answered not, but with a sudden hand
Made bare his branded and ensanguined brow,
Which was like Cain's or Christ's—oh that it should be so!

## XXXV

What softer voice is hushed over the dead?
    Athwart what brow is that dark mantle thrown?
What form leans sadly o'er the white death-bed,
    In mockery of monumental stone,
    The heavy heart heaving without a moan?
If it be he who, gentlest of the wise,
    Taught, soothed, loved, honoured, the departed one,
Let me not vex with inharmonious sighs
The silence of that heart's accepted sacrifice.

## XXXVI

Our Adonais has drunk poison—oh
    What deaf and viperous murderer could crown
Life's early cup with such a draught of woe?
    The nameless worm would now itself disown;
    It felt, yet could escape, the magic tone
Whose prelude held all envy, hate, and wrong,
    But what was howling in one breast alone,
Silent with expectation of the song
Whose master's hand is cold, whose silver lyre unstrung.

## XXXVII

Live thou, whose infamy is not thy fame!
    Live! fear no heavier chastisement from me,
Thou noteless blot on a remembered name!
    But be thyself, and know thyself to be!
    And ever at thy season be thou free
To spill the venom which thy fangs o'erflow:
    Remorse and self-contempt shall cling to thee,
Hot shame shall burn upon thy secret brow,
And like a beaten hound tremble thou shalt—as now.

## XXXVIII

Nor let us weep that our delight is fled
    Far from these carrion-kites that scream below.
He wakes or sleeps with the enduring dead;
    Thou canst not soar where he is sitting now.
    Dust to the dust: but the pure spirit shall flow
Back to the burning fountain whence he came,
    A portion of the Eternal, which must glow
Through time and change, unquenchably the same,
Whilst thy cold embers choke the sordid hearth of shame.

## XXXIX

Peace, peace! he is not dead, he doth not sleep!
    He hath awakened from the dream of life.
'Tis we who, lost in stormy visions, keep
    With phantoms an unprofitable strife,
    And in mad trance strike with our spirit's knife
Invulnerable nothings. We decay
    Like corpses in a charnel; fear and grief
Convulse us and consume us day by day,
And cold hopes swarm like worms within our living clay.

# PERCY BYSSHE SHELLEY

## XL

He has outsoared the shadow of our night.
   Envy and calumny and hate and pain,
And that unrest which men miscall delight,
   Can touch him not and torture not again.
   From the contagion of the world's slow stain
He is secure; and now can never mourn
   A heart grown cold, a head grown grey in vain—
Nor, when the spirit's self has ceased to burn,
With sparkless ashes load an unlamented urn.

## XLI

He lives, he wakes—'tis Death is dead, not he;
   Mourn not for Adonais.—Thou young Dawn,
Turn all thy dew to splendour, for from thee
   The spirit thou lamentest is not gone!
   Ye caverns and ye forests, cease to moan!
Cease, ye faint flowers and fountains! and, thou Air,
   Which like a mourning-veil thy scarf hadst thrown
O'er the abandoned Earth, now leave it bare
Even to the joyous stars which smile on its despair!

## XLII

He is made one with Nature. There is heard
   His voice in all her music, from the moan
Of thunder to the song of night's sweet bird.
   He is a presence to be felt and known
   In darkness and in light, from herb and stone,—
Spreading itself where'er that Power may move
   Which has withdrawn his being to its own,
Which wields the world with never-wearied love,
Sustains it from beneath, and kindles it above.

## XLIII

He is a portion of the loveliness
    Which once he made more lovely. He doth bear
His part, while the One Spirit's plastic stress
    Sweeps through the dull dense world; compelling there
    All new successions to the forms they wear;
Torturing the unwilling dross, that checks its flight,
    To its own likeness, as each mass may bear;
    And bursting in its beauty and its might
From trees and beasts and men into the heaven's light.

## XLIV

The splendours of the firmament of time
    May be eclipsed, but are extinguished not;
Like stars to their appointed height they climb,
    And death is a low mist which cannot blot
    The brightness it may veil. When lofty thought
Lifts a young heart above its mortal lair
    And love and life contend in it for what
Shall be its earthly doom, the dead live there,
And move like winds of light on dark and stormy air.

## XLV

The inheritors of unfulfilled renown
    Rose from their thrones, built beyond mortal thought
Far in the unapparent. Chatterton
    Rose pale, his solemn agony had not
    Yet faded from him: Sidney, as he fought,
And as he fell, and as he lived and loved,
    Sublimely mild, a spirit without spot,
Arose; And Lucan, by his death approved;—
Oblivion as they rose shrank like a thing reproved.

### XLVI

And many more, whose names on earth are dark,
    But whose transmitted effluence cannot die
So long as fire outlives the parent spark,
    Rose, robed in dazzling immortality.
    'Thou art become as one of us,' they cry;
'It was for thee yon kingless sphere has long
    Swung blind in unascended majesty,
Silent alone amid an heaven of song.
Assume thy wingèd throne, thou Vesper of our throng!'

### XLVII

Who mourns for Adonais? Oh come forth,
    Fond wretch, and know thyself and him aright.
Clasp with thy panting soul the pendulous earth;
    As from a centre, dart thy spirit's light
    Beyond all worlds, until its spacious might
Satiate the void circumference: then shrink
    Even to a point within our day and night;
And keep thy heart light, lest it make thee sink,
When hope has kindled hope, and lured thee to the brink

### XLVIII

Or go to Rome, which is the sepulchre,
    Oh not of him, but of our joy. 'Tis nought
That ages, empires, and religions, there
    Lie buried in the ravage they have wrought;
    For such as he can lend—they borrow not
Glory from those who made the world their prey;
    And he is gathered to the kings of thought
Who waged contention with their time's decay,
And of the past are all that cannot pass away.

PERCY BYSSHE SHELLEY

## XLIX

Go thou to Rome,—at once the paradise,
　The grave, the city, and the wilderness;
And where its wrecks like shattered mountains rise,
　And flowering weeds and fragrant copses dress
　The bones of Desolation's nakedness,
Pass, till the Spirit of the spot shall lead
　Thy footsteps to a slope of green access,
Where, like an infant's smile, over the dead
A light of laughing flowers along the grass is spread.

## L

And grey walls moulder round, on which dull Time
　Feeds, like slow fire upon a hoary brand;
And one keen pyramid with wedge sublime,
　Pavilioning the dust of him who planned
　This refuge for his memory, doth stand
Like flame transformed to marble; and beneath
　A field is spread, on which a newer band
Have pitched in heaven's smile their camp of death,
Welcoming him we lose with scarce-extinguished breath.

## LI

Here pause. These graves are all too young as yet
　To have outgrown the sorrow which consigned
Its charge to each; and, if the seal is set
　Here on one fountain of a mourning mind,
　Break it not thou! too surely shalt thou find
Thine own well full, if thou returnest home,
　Of tears and gall. From the world's bitter wind
Seek shelter in the shadow of the tomb.
What Adonais is why fear we to become?

[229

## LII

The One remains, the many change and pass;
    Heaven's light for ever shines, earth's shadows fly;
Life, like a dome of many-coloured glass,
    Stains the white radiance of eternity,
    Until Death tramples it to fragments.—Die,
If thou wouldst be with that which thou dost seek!
    Follow where all is fled!—Rome's azure sky,
Flowers, ruins, statues, music, words, are weak
The glory they transfuse with fitting truth to speak.

## LIII

Why linger, why turn back, why shrink, my heart?
    Thy hopes are gone before: from all things here
They have departed; thou shouldst now depart.
    A light is past from the revolving year,
    And man and woman; and what still is dear
Attracts to crush, repels to make thee wither.
    The soft sky smiles, the low wind whispers near:
'Tis Adonais calls! Oh hasten thither!
No more let life divide what death can join together.

## LIV

That light whose smile kindles the universe,
    That beauty in which all things work and move,
That benediction which the eclipsing curse
    Of birth can quench not, that sustaining Love
    Which, through the web of being blindly wove
By man and beast and earth and air and sea,
    Burns bright or dim, as each are mirrors of
The fire for which all thirst, now beams on me,
Consuming the last clouds of cold mortality.

## LV

The breath whose might I have invoked in song
    Descends on me; my spirit's bark is driven
Far from the shore, far from the trembling throng
    Whose sails were never to the tempest given.
    The massy earth and spherèd skies are riven!
I am borne darkly, fearfully afar!
    Whilst, burning through the inmost veil of heaven,
The soul of Adonais, like a star,
Beacons from the abode where the Eternal are.

## To Night

### I

Swiftly walk over the western wave,
      Spirit of Night!
Out of the misty eastern cave
  Where, all the long and lone daylight,
Thou wovest dreams of joy and fear
Which make thee terrible and dear,
      Swift be thy flight!

### II

Wrap thy form in a mantle grey,
      Star-inwrought;
Blind with thine hair the eyes of Day;
  Kiss her until she be wearied out.
Then wander o'er city and sea and land,
Touching all with thine opiate wand—
      Come, long-sought!

### III

When I arose and saw the dawn,
      I sighed for thee;
When light rode high, and the dew was gone,
  And noon lay heavy on flower and tree,
And the weary Day turned to his rest,
Lingering like an unloved guest,
      I sighed for thee.

## IV

Thy brother Death came, and cried,
      'Wouldst thou me?'
Thy sweet child Sleep, the filmy-eyed,
   Murmured like a noontide bee,
'Shall I nestle near thy side?
Wouldst thou me?'—And I replied,
      'No, not thee.'

## V

Death will come when thou art dead,
      Soon, too soon—
Sleep will come when thou art fled.
   Of neither would I ask the boon.
I ask of thee, beloved Night—
Swift be thine approaching flight,
      Come, soon, soon!

*Lines*

## I

The cold earth slept below,
　　Above the cold sky shone;
And all around with a chilling sound,
　　From caves of ice and fields of snow
　　The breath of night like death did flow
　　　　Beneath the sinking moon.

## II

The wintry hedge was black,
　　The green grass was not seen,
The birds did rest on the bare thorn's breast,
　　Whose roots, beside the pathway track,
　　Had bound their folds o'er many a crack
　　　　Which the frost had made between.

## III

Thine eyes glowed in the glare
　　Of the moon's dying light;
As a fen-fire's beam on a sluggish stream
　　Gleams dimly, so the moon shone there.
　　And it yellowed the strings of thy raven hair,
　　　　That shook in the wind of night.

## IV

The moon made thy lips pale, beloved—
   The wind made thy bosom chill—
The night did shed on thy dear head
  Its frozen dew, and thou didst lie
  Where the bitter breath of the naked sky
    Might visit thee at will.

# PERCY BYSSHE SHELLEY

*On Fanny Godwin*

> Her voice did quiver as we parted,
>     Yet knew I not that heart was broken
> From which it came, and I departed
>     Heeding not the words then spoken.
>         Misery—O Misery,
>             This word is all too wide for thee.

PERCY  BYSSHE  SHELLEY

## To William Shelley

> Thy little footsteps on the sands
>   Of a remote and lonely shore;
> The twinkling of thine infant hands,
>   Where now the worm will feed no more;
> Thy mingled look of love and glee
> When we returned to gaze on thee—

## *The* Waning Moon

And like a dying lady, lean and pale,
Who totters forth, wrapped in a gauzy veil,
Out of the chamber, led by the insane
And feeble wanderings of her fading brain,
The moon arose up in the murky East,
A white and shapeless mass—

## To the Moon

### I

Art thou pale for weariness
Of climbing heaven and gazing on the earth,
　　Wandering companionless
Among the stars that have a different birth,—
And ever changing, like a joyless eye
That finds no object worth its constancy?

### II

Thou chosen sister of the Spirit,
That gazes on thee till in thee it pities. . . .

# PERCY BYSSHE SHELLEY

*Lines Written on Hearing the News of the Death of Napoleon*

What! alive and so bold, O Earth?
  Art thou not overbold?
  What! leapest thou forth as of old
In the light of thy morning mirth,
The last of the flock of the starry fold?
Ha! leapest thou forth as of old?
Are not the limbs still when the ghost is fled,
And canst thou move, Napoleon being dead?

How! is not thy quick heart cold?
  What spark is alive on thy hearth?
How! is not *his* death-knell knolled?
  And livest *thou* still, Mother Earth?
Thou wert warming thy fingers old
O'er the embers covered and cold
Of that most fiery spirit, when it fled—
What, Mother, do you laugh now he is dead?

'Who has known me of old,' replied Earth,
  'Or who has my story told?
  It is thou who art overbold.'
And the lightning of scorn laughed forth
As she sung, 'To my bosom I fold
All my sons when their knell is knolled,
And so with living motion all are fed,
And the quick spring like weeds out of the dead.

'Still alive and still bold,' shouted Earth,
   'I grow bolder and still more bold.
   The dead fill me ten thousandfold
Fuller of speed, and splendour, and mirth.
I was cloudy, and sullen, and cold,
Like a frozen chaos uprolled,
Till by the spirit of the mighty dead
My heart grew warm. I feed on whom I fed.

'Ay, alive and still bold,' muttered Earth,
   'Napoleon's fierce spirit rolled,
   In terror, and blood, and gold,
A torrent of ruin to death from his birth.
Leave the millions who follow to mould
The metal before the cold;
And weave into his shame, which like the dead
Shrouds me, the hopes that from his glory fled.'

# PERCY BYSSHE SHELLEY

## A Lament

### I

O world! O life! O time!
On whose last steps I climb,
   Trembling at that where I had stood before;
When will return the glory of your prime?
    No more—Oh, never more!

### II

Out of the day and night
A joy has taken flight;
Fresh spring, and summer, and winter hoar,
Move my faint heart with grief, but with delight
    No more—Oh, never more.

# PERCY BYSSHE SHELLEY

[From] *Ginevra*

She is still, she is cold
      On the bridal couch,
One step to the white deathbed,
      And one to the bier,
And one to the charnel—and one, oh where?
      The dark arrow fled
      In the noon.

Ere the sun through heaven once more has rolled,
The rats in her heart
Will have made their nest,
And the worms be alive in her golden hair,
While the Spirit that guides the sun,
Sits throned in his flaming chair,
      She shall sleep.

## *To Jane: The Recollection*

### I

Now the last day of many days,
   All beautiful and bright as thou,
      The loveliest and the last, is dead,
Rise, Memory, and write its praise!
     Up,—to thy wonted work! come, trace
      The epitaph of glory fled,—
For now the Earth has changed its face,
   A frown is on the Heaven's brow.

### II

We wandered to the Pine Forest
   That skirts the Ocean's foam,
The lightest wind was in the nest,
   The tempest in its home.
The whispering waves were half asleep,
   The clouds were gone to play,
And on the bosom of the deep
   The smile of Heaven lay;
It seemed as if the hour were one
   Sent from beyond the skies,
Which scattered from above the sun
   A light of Paradise.

### III

We paused amid the pines that stood
    The giants of the waste,
Tortured by storms to shapes as rude
    As serpents interlaced,
And soothed by every azure breath,
    That under Heaven is blown,
To harmonies and hues beneath,
    As tender as its own;
Now all the tree-tops lay asleep,
    Like green waves on the sea,
As still as in the silent deep
    The ocean woods may be.

### IV

How calm it was!—the silence there
    By such a chain was bound
That even the busy woodpecker
    Made stiller by her sound
The inviolable quietness;
    The breath of peace we drew
With its soft motion made not less
    The calm that round us grew.
There seemed from the remotest seat
    Of the white mountain waste,
To the soft flower beneath our feet,
    A magic circle traced,—
A spirit interfused around,
    A thrilling, silent life,—
To momentary peace it bound
    Our mortal nature's strife;

And still I felt the centre of
  The magic circle there
Was one fair form that filled with love
  The lifeless atmosphere.


## V

We paused beside the pools that lie
  Under the forest bough,—
Each seemed as 'twere a little sky
  Gulfed in a world below;
A firmament of purple light
  Which in the dark earth lay,
More boundless than the depth of night,
  And purer than the day—
In which the lovely forests grew,
  As in the upper air,
More perfect both in shape and hue
  Than any spreading there.
There lay the glade and neighbouring lawn
  And through the dark green wood
The white sun twinkling like the dawn
  Out of a speckled cloud.
Sweet views which in our world above
  Can never well be seen,
Were imaged by the water's love
  Of that fair forest green.
And all was interfused beneath
  With an Elysian glow,
An atmosphere without a breath,
  A softer day below.

Like one beloved the scene had lent
   To the dark water's breast,
Its every leaf and lineament
   With more than truth expressed;
Until an envious wind crept by
   Like an unwelcome thought,
Which from the mind's too faithful eye
   Blots one dear image out.
Though thou art ever fair and kind
   The forests ever green,
Less oft is peace in Shelley's mind,
   Than calm in waters, seen.

# PERCY BYSSHE SHELLEY

[From] *Alastor*

> —As an eagle grasped
> In folds of the green serpent, feels her breast
> Burn with the poison, and precipitates
> Through night and day, tempest, and calm, and cloud,
> Frantic with dizzying anguish, her blind flight
> O'er the wide aëry wilderness: thus driven
> By the bright shadow of that lovely dream,
> Beneath the cold glare of the desolate night,
> Through tangled swamps and deep precipitous dells,
> Startling with careless step the moonlight snake,
> He fled.

> .    .    .    .    .    .    .    .    .    .    .

> —'O stream!
> Whose source is inaccessibly profound,
> Whither do thy mysterious waters tend?
> Thou imagest my life. Thy darksome stillness,
> Thy dazzling waves, thy loud and hollow gulfs,
> Thy searchless fountain, and invisible course
> Have each their type in me: and the wide sky,
> And measureless ocean may declare as soon
> What oozy cavern or what wandering cloud
> Contains thy waters, as the universe
> Tell where these living thoughts reside, when stretched
> Upon thy flowers my bloodless limbs shall waste
> I' the passing wind!'

# PERCY BYSSHE SHELLEY

.    .    .    .    .    .    .    .    .    .

           On every side now rose
Rocks, which, in unimaginable forms,
Lifted their black and barren pinnacles
In the light of the evening, and, its precipice
Obscuring the ravine, disclosed above,
Mid toppling stones, black gulfs and yawning caves,
Whose windings gave ten thousand various tongues
To the loud stream. Lo! where the pass expands
Its stony jaws, the abrupt mountain breaks,
And seems, with its accumulated crags,
To overhang the world: for wide expand
Beneath the wan stars and descending moon
Islanded seas, blue mountains, mighty streams,
Dim tracts and vast, robed in the lustrous gloom
Of leaden-coloured even, and fiery hills
Mingling their flames with twilight, on the verge
Of the remote horizon.

.    .    .    .    .    .    .    .    .    .

          —his last sight
Was the great moon, which o'er the western line
Of the wide world her mighty horn suspended,
With whose dun beams inwoven darkness seemed
To mingle.

# PERCY BYSSHE SHELLEY

[From] *The Revolt of Islam*

## [From] Canto I

### VI

I could not choose but gaze; a fascination
    Dwelt in that moon, and sky, and clouds, which drew
My fancy thither, and in expectation
    Of what I knew not, I remained:—the hue
    Of the white moon, amid that heaven so blue,
Suddenly stained with shadow did appear;
    A speck, a cloud, a shape approaching grew,
Like a great ship in the sun's sinking sphere
Beheld afar at sea, and swift it came anear.

### VII

Even like a bark, which from a chasm of mountains,
    Dark, vast, and overhanging, on a river
Which there collects the strength of all its fountains,
    Comes forth, whilst with the speed its frame do
        quiver,
    Sails, oars, and stream, tending to one endeavour;
So, from that chasm of light a wingèd Form
    On all the winds of heaven approaching ever
Floated, dilating as it came: the storm
Pursued it with fierce blasts, and lightnings swift and war

## VIII

A course precipitous, of dizzy speed,
  Suspending thought and breath; a monstrous sight!
For in the air do I behold indeed
  An Eagle and a Serpent wreathed in fight:—
  And now relaxing its impetuous flight,
Before the aërial rock on which I stood,
  The Eagle, hovering, wheeled to left and right,
And hung with lingering wings over the flood,
And startled with its yells the wide air's solitude.

## IX

A shaft of light upon its wings descended,
  And every golden feather gleamed therein—
Feather and scale, inextricably blended.
  The Serpent's mailed and many-coloured skin
  Shone through the plumes its coils were twined within
By many a swoln and knotted fold, and high
  And far, the neck, receding lithe and thin,
Sustained a crested head, which warily
Shifted and glanced before the Eagle's steadfast eye.

## X

Around, around, in ceaseless circles wheeling
  With clang of wings and scream, the Eagle sailed
Incessantly—sometimes on high concealing
  Its lessening orbs, sometimes as if it failed,
  Drooped through the air; and still it shrieked and wailed,
And casting back its eager head, with beak
  And talon unremittingly assailed
The wreathed Serpent, who did ever seek
Upon his enemy's heart a mortal wound to wreak.

PERCY BYSSHE SHELLEY

## XI

What life, what power, was kindled and arose
   Within the sphere of that appalling fray!
For, from the encounter of those wondrous foes,
   A vapour like the sea's suspended spray
   Hung gathered: in the void air, far away,
Floated the shattered plumes; bright scales did leap,
   Where'er the Eagle's talons made their way,
Like sparks into the darkness;—as they sweep,
Blood stains the snowy foam of the tumultuous deep.

## XII

Swift chances in that combat—many a check,
   And many a change, a dark and wild turmoil;
Sometimes the Snake around his enemy's neck
   Locked in stiff rings his adamantine coil,
   Until the Eagle, faint with pain and toil,
Remitted his strong flight, and near the sea
   Languidly fluttered, hopeless so to foil
His adversary, who then reared on high
His red and burning crest, radiant with victory.

## XIII

Then on the white edge of the bursting surge,
   Where they had sunk together, would the Snake
Relax his suffocating grasp, and scourge
   The wind with his wild writhings; for to break
   That chain of torment, the vast bird would shake
The strength of his unconquerable wings
   As in despair, and with his sinewy neck,
Dissolve in sudden shock those linked rings,
Then soar—as swift as smoke from a volcano springs.

## XIV

Wile baffled wile, and strength encountered strength,
 Thus long, but unprevailing:—the event
Of that portentous fight appeared at length:
 Until the lamp of day was almost spent
 It had endured, when lifeless, stark, and rent,
Hung high that mighty Serpent, and at last
 Fell to the sea, while o'er the continent,
With clang of wings and scream the Eagle passed,
Heavily borne away on the exhausted blast.

[From] Canto III

The islands and the mountains in the day
    Like clouds reposed afar; and I could see
The town among the woods below that lay,
And the dark rocks which bound the bright and glassy ba

### XVI

It was so calm, that scarce the feathery weed
    Sown by some eagle on the topmost stone
Swayed in the air:—

.    .    .    .    .    .    .    .

# PERCY BYSSHE SHELLEY

[*From*] Canto III

## XXVII

Then seemed it that a tameless hurricane
    Arose, and bore me in its dark career
Beyond the sun, beyond the stars that wane
    On the verge of formless space—it languished there,
    And dying, left a silence lone and drear,
More horrible than famine:—in the deep
    The shape of an old man did then appear,
Stately and beautiful; that dreadful sleep
His heavenly smiles dispersed, and I could wake and weep.

## XXVIII

And, when the blinding tears had fallen, I saw
    That column, and those corpses, and the moon,
And felt the poisonous tooth of hunger gnaw
    My vitals, I rejoiced, as if the boon
    Of senseless death would be accorded soon;—
When from that stony gloom a voice arose,
    Solemn and sweet as when low winds attune
The midnight pines; the grate did then unclose,
And on that reverend form the moonlight did repose.

## XXIX

He struck my chains, and gently spake and smiled:
    As they were loosened by that Hermit old,

[255

Mine eyes were of their madness half beguiled,
  To answer those kind looks—he did enfold
  His giant arms around me, to uphold
My wretched frame, my scorchèd limbs he wound
  In linen moist and balmy, and as cold
As dew to drooping leaves;—the chain, with sound
Like earthquake, through the chasm of that steep stair di
  bound,


                    XXX

As, lifting me, it fell!—What next I heard,
  Were billows leaping on the harbour-bar,
And the shrill sea-wind, whose breath idly stirred
  My hair;—I looked abroad, and saw a star
  Shining beside a sail, and distant far
That mountain and its column, the known mark
  Of those who in the wide deep wandering are,
So that I feared some Spirit, fell and dark,
In trance had lain me thus within a fiendish bark.


                    XXXI

For now indeed, over the salt sea-billow
  I sailed: Yet dared not look upon the shape
Of him who ruled the helm, although the pillow
  For my light head was hollowed in his lap,
  And my bare limbs his mantle did enwrap,
  Fearing it was a fiend: at last, he bent
  O'er me his aged face, as if to snap
Those dreadful thoughts the gentle grandsire bent,
And to my inmost soul his soothing looks he sent.

## XXXII

A soft and healing potion to my lips
    At intervals he raised—now looked on high,
To mark if yet the starry giant dips
    His zone in the dim sea—now cheeringly,
    Though he said little, did he speak to me.
'It is a friend beside thee—take good cheer,
    Poor victim, thou art now at liberty!'
I joyed as those a human tone to hear,
Who in cells deep and lone have languished many a year.

## [From] Canto V

### XIV

Lifting the thunder of their acclamation,
   Towards the City then the multitude,
And I among them, went in joy—a nation
   Made free by love;—a mighty brotherhood
   Linked by a jealous interchange of good;
A glorious pageant, more magnificent
   Than kingly slaves arrayed in gold and blood,
When they return from carnage, and are sent
In triumph bright beneath the populous battlement.

### XV

Afar, the city-walls were thronged on high,
   And myriads on each giddy turret clung,
And to each spire far lessening in the sky
   Bright pennons on the idle winds were hung;
   As we approached, a shout of joyance sprung
At once from all the crowd, as if the vast
   And peopled Earth its boundless skies among
The sudden clamour of delight had cast,
When from before its face some general wreck had passe

### XVI

Our armies through the City's hundred gates
   Were poured, like brooks which to the rocky lair

Of some deep lake, whose silence them awaits,
    Throng from the mountains when the storms are there
    And, as we passed through the calm sunny air
A thousand flower-inwoven crowns were shed,
    The token flowers of truth and freedom fair,
And fairest hands bound them on many a head,
Those angels of love's heaven, that over all was spread.

## XVII

I trod as one tranced in some rapturous vision:
    Those bloody bands so lately reconciled,
Were, ever as they went, by the contrition
    Of anger turned to love, from ill beguiled,
    And every one of them more gently smiled,
Because they had done evil:—the sweet awe
    Of such mild looks made their own hearts grow mild,
And did with soft attraction ever draw
Their spirits to the love of freedom's equal law.

# PERCY BYSSHE SHELLEY

[From] *Prometheus Unbound*

[*From*] Act I

On a poet's lips I slept
Dreaming like a love-adept
In the sound his breathing kept;
Nor seeks nor finds he mortal blisses,
But feeds on the aërial kisses
Of shapes that haunt thought's wildernesses.
He will watch from dawn to gloom
The lake-reflected sun illume
The yellow bees in the ivy-bloom,
Nor heed nor see, what things they be;
But from these create he can
Forms more real than living man,
Nurslings of immortality!
One of these awakened me,
And I sped to succour thee.

[*From*] Act III, Scene II

Ocean

The loud deep calls me home even now to feed it
With azure calm out of the emerald urns
Which stand for ever full beside my throne.
Behold the Nereids under the green sea,
Their wavering limbs borne on the wind-like stream,
Their white arms lifted o'er their streaming hair
With garlands pied and starry sea-flower crowns,
Hastening to grace their mighty sister's joy.
It is the unpastured sea hungering for calm.

# PERCY BYSSHE SHELLEY

### [From] Act III, Scene IV

#### Spirit of the Hour

Soon as the sound had ceased whose thunder filled
The abysses of the sky and the wide earth,
There was a change: the impalpable thin air
And the all-circling sunlight were transformed,
As if the sense of love dissolved in them
Had folded itself round the sphèrèd world.
My vision then grew clear, and I could see
Into the mysteries of the universe:
Dizzy as with delight I floated down,
Winnowing the lightsome air with languid plumes,
My coursers sought their birthplace in the sun,
Where they henceforth will live exempt from toil,
Pasturing flowers of vegetable fire;
And where my moonlike car will stand within
A temple, gazed upon by Phidian forms
Of thee, and Asia, and the Earth, and me,
And you fair nymphs looking the love we feel,—
In memory of the tidings it has borne,—
Beneath a dome fretted with graven flowers,
Poised on twelve columns of resplendent stone,
And open to the bright and liquid sky.
Yoked to it by an amphisbænic snake
The likeness of those wingèd steeds will mock
The flight from which they find repose. Alas,

Whither has wandered now my partial tongue
When all remains untold which ye would hear?
As I have said, I floated to the earth:
It was, as it is still, the pain of bliss
To move, to breathe, to be; I wandering went
Among the haunts and dwellings of mankind,
And first was disappointed not to see
Such mighty change as I had felt within
Expressed in outward things; but soon I looked,
And behold, thrones were kingless, and men walked
One with the other even as spirits do.
None fawned, none trampled; hate, disdain, or fear,
Self-love or self-contempt, on human brows
No more inscribed, as o'er the gate of hell,
"All hope abandon ye who enter here";
None frowned, none trembled, none with eager fear
Gazed on another's eye of cold command,
Until the subject of a tyrant's will
Became, worse fate, the abject of his own,
Which spurred him, like an outspent horse, to death.
None wrought his lips in truth-entangling lines
Which smiled the lie his tongue disdained to speak;
None, with firm sneer, trod out in his own heart
The sparks of love and hope till there remained
Those bitter ashes, a soul self-consumed,
And the wretch crept a vampire among man,
Infecting all with his own hideous ill;
None talked that common, false, cold, hollow talk
Which makes the heart deny the yes it breathes,
Yet question that unmeant hypocrisy
With such a self-mistrust as has no name.

# PERCY BYSSHE SHELLEY

And women, too, frank, beautiful, and kind
As the free heaven which rains fresh light and dew
On the wide earth, past; gentle radiant forms,
From custom's evil taint exempt and pure;
Speaking the wisdom once they could not think,
Looking emotions once they feared to feel,
And changed to all which once they dared not be,
Yet being now, made earth like heaven; nor pride,
Nor jealousy, nor envy, nor ill shame,
The bitterest of those drops of treasured gall,
Spoilt the sweet taste of the nepenthe, love.

Thrones, altars, judgement-seats, and prisons; wherein,
And beside which, by wretched men were borne
Sceptres, tiaras, swords, and chains, and tomes
Of reasoned wrong, glozed on by ignorance,
Were like those monstrous and barbaric shapes,
The ghosts of a no-more-remembered fame,
Which, from their unworn obelisks, look forth
In triumph o'er the palaces and tombs
Of those who were their conquerors: mouldering round,
These imaged to the pride of kings and priests
A dark yet mighty faith, a power as wide
As is the world it wasted, and are now
But an astonishment; even so the tools
And emblems of its last captivity,
Amid the dwellings of the peopled earth,
Stand, not o'erthrown, but unregarded now.
And those foul shapes, abhorred by god and man,—
Which, under many a name and many a form
Strange, savage, ghastly, dark and execrable,

Were Jupiter, the tyrant of the world;
And which the nations, panic-stricken, served
With blood, and hearts broken by long hope, and love
Dragged to his altars soiled and garlandless,
And slain amid men's unreclaiming tears,
Flattering the thing they feared, which fear was hate,—
Frown, mouldering fast, o'er their abandoned shrines:
The painted veil, by those who were, called life,
Which mimicked, as with colours idly spread,
All men believed or hoped, is torn aside;
The loathsome mask has fallen, the man remains
Sceptreless, free, uncircumscribed, but man
Equal, unclassed, tribeless, and nationless,
Exempt from awe, worship, degree, the king
Over himself; just, gentle, wise: but man
Passionless?—no, yet free from guilt or pain,
Which were, for his will made or suffered them,
Nor yet exempt, though ruling them like slaves,
From chance, and death, and mutability,
The clogs of that which else might oversoar
The loftiest star of unascended heaven,
Pinnacled dim in the intense inane.

# PERCY BYSSHE SHELLEY

[From] *Peter Bell the Third*

## Part the Fifth

### Grace

#### I

Among the guests who often stayed
   Till the Devil's petits-soupers.
A man there came, fair as a maid,
And Peter noted what he said,
   Standing behind his master's chair.

#### II

He was a mighty poet—and
   A subtle-souled psychologist;
All things he seemed to understand,
Of old or new—of sea or land—
   But his own mind—which was a mist.

#### III

This was a man who might have turned
   Hell into Heaven—and so in gladness
A Heaven unto himself have earned;
But he in shadows undiscerned
   Trusted—and damned himself to madness.

IV

He spoke of poetry, and how
    'Divine it was—a light—a love—
A spirit which like wind doth blow
As it listeth, to and fro;
    A dew rained down from God above;


V

'A power which comes and goes like dream,
    And which none can ever trace—
Heaven's light on earth—Truth's brightest beam.'
And when he ceased there lay the gleam
    Of those words upon his face.


VI

Now Peter, when he heard such talk,
    Would, heedless of a broken pate,
Stand like a man asleep, or balk
Some wishing guest of knife or fork,
    Or drop and break his master's plate.


VII

At night he oft would start and wake
    Like a lover, and began
In a wild measure songs to make
On moor, and glen, and rocky lake,
    And on the heart of man—

## VIII

And on the universal sky—
  And the wide earth's bosom green,—
And the sweet, strange mystery
Of what beyond these things may lie,
  And yet remain unseen.

## IX

For in his thought he visited
  The spots in which, ere dead and damned,
He his wayward life had led;
Yet knew not whence the thoughts were fed
  Which thus his fancy crammed.

## X

And these obscure remembrances
  Stirred such harmony in Peter,
That, whensoever he should please,
He could speak of rocks and trees
  In poetic metre.

## XI

For though it was without a sense
  Of memory, yet he remembered well
Many a ditch and quick-set fence;
Of lakes he had intelligence,
  He knew something of heath and fell.

## XII

He had also dim recollections
　　Of pedlars tramping on their rounds;
Milk-pans and pails; and odd collections
Of saws, and proverbs; and reflections
　　Old parsons make in burying-grounds.

## XIII

But Peter's verse was clear, and came
　　Announcing from the frozen hearth
Of a cold age, that none might tame
The soul of that diviner flame
　　It augured to the Earth:

## XIV

Like gentle rains, on the dry plains,
　　Making that green which late was gray,
Or like the sudden moon, that stains
Some gloomy chamber's window-panes
　　With a broad light like day.

## XV

For language was in Peter's hand
　　Like clay while he was yet a potter;
And he made songs for all the land,
Sweet both to feel and understand,
　　As pipkins late to mountain Cotter.

## XVI

And Mr. ——, the bookseller,
   Gave twenty pounds for some;—then scorning
A footman's yellow coat to wear,
Peter, too proud of heart, I fear,
   Instantly gave the Devil warning.

## XVII

Whereat the Devil took offence,
   And swore in his soul a great oath then,
'That for his damned impertinence
He'd bring him to a proper sense
   Of what was due to gentlemen!'

# PERCY BYSSHE SHELLEY

[From] *Letter to Maria Gisborne*

You are now

In London, that great sea, whose ebb and flow
At once is deaf and loud, and on the shore
Vomits its wrecks, and still howls on for more.
Yet in its depths what treasures! You will see
That which was Godwin,—greater none than he
Though fallen—and fallen on evil times—to stand
Among the spirits of our age and land,
Before the dread tribunal of *to come*
The foremost,—while Rebuke cowers pale and dumb.
You will see Coleridge—he who sits obscure
In the exceeding lustre and the pure
Intense irradiation of a mind,
Which, with its own internal lightning blind,
Flags wearily through darkness and despair—
A cloud-encircled meteor of the air,
A hooded eagle among blinking owls.—
You will see Hunt—one of those happy souls
Which are the salt of the earth, and without whom
This world would smell like what it is—a tomb;
Who is, what others seem; his room no doubt
Is still adorned with many a cast from Shout,
With graceful flowers tastefully placed about;
And coronals of bay from ribbons hung,
The gifts of the most learned among some dozens
Of female friends, sisters-in-law, and cousins.

And there is he with his eternal puns,
Which beat the dullest brain for smiles, like duns
Thundering for money at a poet's door;
Alas! it is no use to say, 'I'm poor!'
Or oft in graver mood, when he will look
Things wiser than were ever read in book,
Except in Shakespeare's wisest tenderness.—
You will see Hogg,—and I cannot express
His virtues,—though I know that they are great,
Because he looks, then barricades the gate
Within which they inhabit;—of his wit
And wisdom, you'll cry out when you are bit.
He is a pearl within an oyster shell,
One of the richest of the deep;—and there
Is English Peacock, with his mountain Fair,
Turned into a Flamingo;—that shy bird
That gleams i' the Indian air—have you not heard
When a man marries, dies, or turns Hindoo,
His best friends hear no more of him?—but you
Will see him, and will like him too, I hope,
With the milk-white Snowdonian Antelope
Matched with this camelopard—his fine wit
Makes such a wound, the knife is lost in it;
A strain to learnèd for a shallow age
Too wise for selfish bigots; let his page,
Which charms to chosen spirits of the time,
Fold itself up for the serener clime
Of years to come, and find its recompense
In that just expectation.—Wit and sense,
Virtue and human knowledge; all that might
Make this dull world a business of delight,

Are all combined in Horace Smith.—And these,
With some exceptions, which I need not tease
Your patience by descanting on,—are all
You and I know in London.

# PERCY BYSSHE SHELLEY

[From] *Epipsychidion*

Spouse! Sister! Angel! Pilot of the Fate
Whose course has been so starless! O too late
Belovèd! O too soon adored by me!
For in the fields of Immortality
My spirit should at first have worshipped thine,
A divine presence in a place divine;
Or should have moved beside it on this earth,
A shadow of that substance, from its birth;
But not as now:—I love thee; yes I feel
That on the fountain of my heart a seal
I set, to keep the waters pure and bright
For thee, since in those *tears* thou hast delight.
We—are we not formed, as notes of music are,
For one another, though dissimilar;
Such difference without discord, as can make
Those sweetest sounds, in which all spirits shake
As trembling leaves in a continuous air?

Thy wisdom speaks in me, and bids me dare
Beacon the rocks on which high hearts are wrecked.
I never was attached to that great sect,
Whose doctrine is, that each one should select
Out of the crowd a mistress or a friend,
And all the rest, though fair and wise, commend
To cold oblivion, though it is in the code
Of modern morals, and the beaten road

Which those poor slaves with weary footsteps tread,
Who travel to their home among the dead
By the broad highway of the world, and so
With one chained friend, perhaps a jealous foe,
The dreariest and the longest journey go.

True love in this differs from gold and clay,
That to divide is not to take away.
Love is like understanding, that grows bright,
Gazing on many truths; 'tis like thy light,
Imagination! which from earth and sky,
And from the depths of human fantasy,
As from a thousand prisms and mirrors fills
The Universe with glorious beams, and kills
Error, the worm, with many a sun-like arrow
Of its reverberated lightning. Narrow
The heart that loves, the brain that contemplates,
The life that wears, the spirit that creates
One object, and one form, and builds thereby
A sepulchre for its eternity.

# PERCY BYSSHE SHELLEY

## The Triumph of Life

Swift as a spirit hastening to his task
Of glory and of good, the Sun sprang forth
Rejoicing in his splendour, and the mask

Of darkness fell from the awakened Earth—
The smokeless altars of the mountain snows
Flamed above crimson clouds, and at the birth

Of light, the Ocean's orison arose,
To which the birds tempered their matin lay.
All flowers in field or forest which unclose

Their trembling eyelids to the kiss of day,
Swinging their censers in the element,
With orient incense lit by the new ray

Burned slow and inconsumably, and sent
Their odorous sighs up to the smiling air;
And, in succession due, did continent,

Isle, ocean, and all things that in them wear
The form and character of mortal mould,
Rise as the Sun their father rose, to bear

Their portion of the toil, which he of old
Took as his own, and then imposed on them:
But I, whom thoughts which must remain untold

Had kept as wakeful as the stars that gem
The cone of night, now they were laid asleep
Stretched my faint limbs beneath the hoary stem

Which an old chestnut flung athwart the steep
Of a green Apennine: before me fled
The night; behind me rose the day; the deep

Was at my feet, and Heaven above my head,—
When a strange trance over my fancy grew
Which was not slumber, for the shade it spread

Was so transparent, that the scene came through
As clear as when a veil of light is drawn
O'er evening hills they glimmer; and I knew

That I had felt the freshness of that dawn
Bathe in the same cold dew my brow and hair,
And sate as thus upon that slope of lawn

Under the self-same bough, and heard as there
The birds, the fountains and the ocean hold
Sweet talk in music through the enamoured air
And then a vision on my brain was rolled.

# PERCY BYSSHE SHELLEY

As in that trance of wondrous thought I lay,
This was the tenour of my waking dream:—
Methought I sate beside a public way

Thick strewn with summer dust; and a great stream
Of people there was hurrying to and fro,
Numerous as gnats upon the evening gleam,

All hastening onward, yet none seemed to know
Whither he went, or whence he came, or why
He made one of the multitude, and so

Was borne amid the crowd, as through the sky
One of the million leaves of summer's bier;
Old age and youth, manhood and infancy,

Mixed in one mighty torrent did appear,
Some flying from the thing they feared, and some
Seeking the object of another's fear;

And others, as with steps towards the tomb,
Pored on the trodden worms that crawled beneath,
And others mournfully within the gloom

Of their own shadow walked, and called it death;
And some fled from it as it were a ghost,
Half fainting in the affliction of vain breath:

But more, with motions which each other crossed,
Pursued or shunned the shadows the clouds threw,
Or birds within the noonday aether lost,

Upon that path where flowers never grew.—
And, weary with vain toil and faint for thirst,
Heard not the fountains, whose melodious dew

Out of their mossy cells forever burst;
Nor felt the breeze which from the forest told
Of grassy paths and wood-lawns interspersed

With overarching elms and caverns cold,
And violet banks where sweet dreams brood, but they
Pursued their serious folly as of old.

And as I gazed, methought that in the way
The throng grew wilder, as the woods of June
When the south wind shakes the extinguished day,

And a cold glare, intenser than the noon,
But icy cold, obscured with blinding light
The sun, as he the stars. Like the young moon—

When on the sunlit limits of the night
Her white shell trembles amid crimson air,
And whilst the sleeping tempest gathers might—

Doth, as the herald of its coming, bear
The ghost of its dead mother, whose dim form
Bends in dark aether from her infant's chair,—

So came a chariot on the silent storm
Of its own rushing splendour, and a Shape
So sate within, as one whom years deform,

# PERCY BYSSHE SHELLEY

Beneath a dusky hood and double cape,
Crouching within the shadow of a tomb;
And o'er what seemed the head of cloud-like crape

Was bent, a dun and faint aethereal gloom
Tempering the light. Upon the chariot-beam
A Janus-visaged Shadow did assume

The guidance of that wonder-wingèd team;
The shapes which drew it in thick lightenings
Were lost:—I heard alone on the air's soft stream

The music of their ever-moving wings.
All the four faces of that Charioteer
Had their eyes banded; little profit brings

Speed in the van and blindness in the rear,
Nor then avail the beams that quench the sun,—
Or that with banded eyes could pierce the sphere

Of all that is, has been or will be done;
So ill was the car guided—but it passed
With solemn speed majestically on.

The crowd gave way, and I arose aghast,
Or seemed to rise, so mighty was the trance,
And saw, like clouds upon the thunder-blast,

The million with fierce song and maniac dance
Raging around—such seemed the jubilee
As when to greet some conqueror's advance

Imperial Rome poured forth her living sea
From senate-house, and forum, and theatre,
When                         upon the free

Had bound a yoke, which soon they stooped to bear.
Nor wanted here the just similitude
Of a triumphal pageant, for where'er

The chariot rolled, a captive multitude
Was driven;—all those who had grown old in power
Or misery,—all who had their age subdued

By action or by suffering, and whose hour
Was drained to its last sand in weal or woe,
So that the trunk survived both fruit and flower;—

All those whose fame or infamy must grow
Till the great winter lay the form and name
Of this green earth with them for ever low;—

All but the sacred few who could not tame
Their spirits to the conquerors—but as soon
As they had touched the world with living flame,

Fled back like eagles to their native noon,
Or those who put aside the diadem
Of earthly thrones or gems . . .

Were there, of Athens or Jerusalem,
Were neither mid the mighty captives seen,
Nor mid the ribald crowd that followed them,

Nor those who went before fierce and obscene.
The wild dance maddens in the van, and those
Who led it—fleet as shadows on the green,

Outspeed the chariot, and without repose
Mix with each other in tempestuous measure
To savage music, wilder as it grows,

They, tortured by their agonizing pleasure,
Convulsed and on the rapid whirlwinds spun
Of that fierce Spirit, whose unholy leisure

Was soothed by mischief since the world begun,
Throw back their heads and loose their streaming hair;
And in their dance round her who dims the sun,

Maidens and youth fling their wild arms in air
As their feet twinkle; they recede, and now
Bending within each other's atmosphere,

Kindle invisibly—and as they glow,
Like moths by light attracted and repelled,
Oft to their bright destruction come and go,

Till like two clouds into one vale impelled,
That shake the mountains when their lightnings mingle
And die in rain—the fiery band which held

Their natures, snaps—while the shock still may tingle:
One falls and then another in the path
Senseless—nor is the desolation single,

Yet ere I can say *where*—the chariot hath
Passed over them—nor other trace I find
But as of foam after the ocean's wrath

Is spent upon the desert shore;—behind,
Old men and women foully disarrayed,
Shake their gray hairs in the insulting wind,

And follow in the dance, with limbs decayed,
Seeking to reach the light which leaves them still
Farther behind and deeper in the shade.

But not the less with impotence of will
They wheel, though ghastly shadows interpose
Round them and round each other, and fulfil

Their work, and in the dust from whence they rose
Sink, and corruption veils them as they lie,
And past in these performs what           in those.

Struck to the heart by this sad pageantry,
Half to myself I said—'And what is this?
Whose shape is that within the car? And why—'

I would have added—'is all here amiss?—'
But a voice answered—'Life!'—I turned, and knew
(O Heaven, have mercy on such wretchedness!)

That what I thought was an old root which grew
To strange distortion out of the hill side,
Was indeed one of those deluded crew,

And that the grass, which methought hung so wide
And white, was but this thin discoloured hair,
And that the holes he vainly sought to hide,

Were or had been eyes:—'If thou canst, forbear
To join the dance, which I had well forborne!'
Said the grim Feature (of my thought aware).

'I will unfold that which to this deep scorn
Led me and my companions, and relate
The progress of the pageant since the morn;

'If thirst of knowledge shall not then abate,
Follow it thou even to the night, but I
Am weary.'—Then like one who with the weight

Of his own words is staggered, wearily
He paused, and ere he could resume, I cried:
'First, who art thou?'—'Before thy memory,

'I feared, loved, hated, suffered, did and died,
And if the spark with which Heaven lit my spirit
Had been with purer nutriment supplied,

'Corruption would not now thus much inherit
Of what was once Rousseau,—nor this disguise
Stain that which ought to have disdained to wear it;

'If I have been extinguished, yet there rise
A thousand beacons from the spark I bore'—
'And who are those chained to the car?'—'The wise,

'The great, the unforgotten,—they who wore
Mitres and helms and crowns, or wreaths of light,
Signs of thought's empire over thought—their lore

'Taught them not this, to know themselves; their might
Could not repress the mystery within,
And for the morn of truth they feigned, deep night

'Caught them ere evening.'—'Who is he with chin
Upon his breast, and hands crossed on his chains?'—
'The child of a fierce hour; he sought to win

'The world, and lost all that it did contain
Of greatness, in its hope destroyed; and more
Of fame and peace than virtue's self can gain

'Without the opportunity which bore
Him on its eagle pinions to the peak
From which a thousand climbers have before

'Fallen as Napoleon fell.'—I felt my cheek
Alter, to see the shadow pass away,
Whose grasp had left the giant world so weak

That every pigmy kicked it as it lay;
And much I grieved to think how power and will
In opposition rule our mortal day,

And why God made irreconcilable
Good and the means of good; and for despair
I half disdained mine eyes' desire to fill

With the spent vision of the times that were
And scarce have ceased to be.—'Dost thou behold,'
Said my guide, 'those spoilers spoiled, Voltaire,

'Frederick, and Paul, Catherine, and Leopold,
And hoary anarchs, demagogues, and sage—
        names which the world thinks always old,

'For in the battle Life and they did wage,
She remained conqueror. I was overcome
By my own heart alone, which neither age,

'Nor tears, nor infamy, nor now the tomb
Could temper to its object.'—'Let them pass,'
I cried, 'the world and its mysterious doom

'Is not so much more glorious than it was,
That I desire to worship those who drew
New figures on its false and fragile glass

'As the old faded.'—'Figures ever new
Rise on the bubble, paint them as you may;
We have but thrown, as those before us threw,

'Our shadows on it as it passed away.
But mark how chained to the triumphal chair
The mighty phantoms of an elder day;

'All that is mortal of great Plato there
Expiates the joy and woe his master knew not;
The star that ruled his doom was far too fair.

'And life, where long that flower of Heaven grew not
Conquered that heart by love, which gold, or pain,
Or age, or sloth, or slavery could subdue not.

'And near him walk the                    twain,
The tutor and his pupil, whom Dominion
Followed as tame as vulture in a chain.

'The world was darkened beneath either pinion
Of him whom from the flock of conquerors
Fame singled out for the thunder-bearing minion;

'The other long outlived both woes and wars,
Throned in the thoughts of men, and still had kept
The jealous key of Truth's eternal doors,

'If Bacon's eagle spirit had not lept
Like lightning out of darkness—he compelled
The Proteus shape of Nature, as it slept

'To wake, and lead him to the caves that held
The treasure of the secrets of its reign.
See the great bards of elder time, who quelled

'The passions which they sung, as by their strain
May well be known: their living melody
Tempers its own contagion to the vein

'Of those who are infected with it—I
Have suffered what I wrote, or viler pain!
And so my words have seeds of misery—

[287

'Even as the deeds of others, not as theirs.'
And then he pointed to a company,

'Midst whom I quickly recognized the heirs
Of Caesar's crime, from him to Constantine;
The anarch chiefs, whose force and murderous snares

Had founded many a sceptre-bearing line,
And spread the plague of gold and blood abroad:
And Gregory and John, and men divine,

Who rose like shadows between man and God;
Till that eclipse, still hanging over heaven,
Was worshipped by the world o'er which they strode,'

For the true sun it quenched—'Their power was given
But to destroy,' replied the leader:—'I
Am one of those who have created, even

If it be but a world of agony.'—
'Whence camest thou? and whither goest thou?
How did thy course begin?' I said, 'and why?

'Mine eyes are sick of this perpetual flow
Of people, and my heart sick of one sad thought—
Speak!'—'Whence I am, I partly seem to know,

'And how and by what paths I have been brought
To this dread pass, methinks even thou mayst guess;—
Why this should be, my mind can compass not;

'Whither the conqueror hurries me, still less;—
But follow thou, and from spectator turn
Actor or victim in this wretchedness,

'And what thou wouldst be taught I then may learn
From thee. Now listen:—In the April prime,
When all the forest-tips began to burn

'With kindling green, touched by the azure clime
Of the young season, I was laid asleep
Under a mountain, which from unknown time

'Had yawned into a cavern, high and deep;
And from it came a gentle rivulet,
Whose water, like clear air, in its calm sweep

'Bent the soft grass, and kept for ever wet
The stems of the sweet flowers, and filled the grove
With sounds, which whoso hears must needs forget

'All pleasure and all pain, all hate and love,
Which they had known before that hour of rest;
A sleeping mother then would dream not of

'Her only child who dies upon the breast
At eventide—a king would mourn no more
The crown of which his brows were dispossessed

'When the sun lingered o'er his ocean floor
To gild his rival's new prosperity.
Thou wouldst forget thus vainly to deplore

'Ills, which if ills can find no cure from thee,
The thought of which no other sleep will quell,
Nor other music blot from memory,

'So sweet and deep is the oblivious spell;
And whether life had been before that sleep
The Heaven which I imagine, or a Hell

'Like this harsh world in which I wake to weep,
I know not. I arose, and for a space
The scene of woods and waters seemed to keep,

'Though it was now broad day, a gentle trace
Of light diviner than the common sun
Sheds on the common earth, and all the place

'Was filled with magic sounds woven into one
Oblivious melody, confusing sense
Amid the gliding waves and shadows dun;

'And as I looked, the bright omnipresence
Of morning through the orient cavern flowed,
And the sun's image radiantly intense

'Burned on the waters of the well that glowed
Like gold, and threaded all the forest's maze
With winding paths of emerald fire; there stood

'Amid the sun, as he amid the blaze
Of his own glory, on the vibrating
Floor of the fountain, paved with flashing rays,

'A Shape all light, which with one hand did fling
Dew on the earth, as if she were the dawn,
And the invisible rain did ever sing

'A silver music on the mossy lawn;
And still before me on the dusky grass,
Iris her many-coloured scarf had drawn:

'In her right hand she bore a crystal glass,
Mantling with bright Nepenthe; the fierce splendour
Fell from her as she moved under the mass

'Of the deep cavern, and with palms so tender,
Their tread broke not the mirror of its billow,
Glided along the river, and did bend her

'Head under the dark boughs, till like a willow
Her fair hair swept the bosom of the stream
That whispered with delight to be its pillow.

'As on enamoured is upborne in dream
O'er lily-paven lakes, mid silver mist,
To wondrous music, so this shape might seem

'Partly to tread the waves with feet which kissed
The dancing foam; partly to glide along
The air which roughened the moist amethyst,

'Or the faint morning beams that fell among
The trees, or the soft shadows of the trees;
And her feet, ever to the ceaseless song

# PERCY BYSSHE SHELLEY

'Of leaves, and winds, and waves, and birds, and bees,
And falling drops, moved in a measure new
Yet sweet, as on the summer evening breeze,

'Up from the lake a shape of golden dew
Between two rocks, athwart the rising moon,
Dances i' the wind, where never eagle flew;

'And still her feet, no less than the sweet tune
To which they moved, seemed as they moved to blot
The thoughts of him who gazed on them; and soon

'All that was, seemed as if it had been not;
And all the gazer's mind was strewn beneath
Her feet like embers; and she, thought by thought,

'Trampled its sparks into the dust of death;
As day upon the threshold of the east
Treads out the lamps of night, until the breath

'Of darkness re-illumine even the least
Of heaven's living eyes—like day she came,
Making the night a dream; and ere she ceased

'To move, as one between desire and shame
Suspended, I said—If, as it doth seem,
Thou comest from the realm without a name

'Into this valley of perpetual dream,
Show whence I came, and where I am, and why—
Pass not away upon the passing stream.

'Arise and quench thy thirst, was her reply.
And as a shut lily stricken by the wand
Of dewy morning's vital alchemy,

'I rose; and, bending at her sweet command,
Touched with faint lips the cup she raised,
And suddenly my brain became a sand

'Where the first wave had more than half erased
The track of deer on desert Labrador;
Whilst the wolf, from which they fled amazed,

'Leaves his stamp visibly upon the shore,
Until the second burst;—so on my sight
Burst a new vision, never seen before,

'And the fair shape waned in the coming light,
As veil by veil the silent splendour drops
From Lucifer, amid the chrysolite

'Of sunrise, ere it tinge the mountain-tops;
And as the presence of that fairest planet,
Although unseen, is felt by one who hopes

'That his day's path may end as he began it,
In that star's smile, whose light is like the scent
Of a jonquil when evening breezes fan it,

'Or the soft note in which his dear lament
The Brescian shepherd breathes, or the caress
That turned his weary slumber to content;

'So knew I in that light's severe excess
The presence of that Shape which on the stream
Moved, as I moved along the wilderness,

'More dimly than a day-appearing dream,
The ghost of a forgotten form of sleep;
A light of heaven, whose half-extinguished beam

'Through the sick day in which we wake to weep
Glimmers, for ever sought, for ever lost;
So did that shape its obscure tenour keep

'Beside my path, as silent as a ghost;
But the new Vision, and the cold bright car,
With solemn speed and stunning music, crossed

'The forest, and as if from some dread war
Triumphantly returning, the loud million
Fiercely extolled the fortune of her star.

'A moving arch of victory, the vermilion
And green and azure plumes of Iris had
Built high over her wind-wingèd pavilion,

'And underneath aethereal glory clad
The wilderness, and far before her flew
The tempest of the splendour, which forbade

'Shadow to fall from leaf and stone; the crew
Seemed in that light, like atomies to dance
Within a sunbeam;—some upon the new

'Embroidery of flowers, that did enhance
The grassy vesture of the desert, played,
Forgetful of the chariot's swift advance;

'Others stood gazing, till within the shade
Of the great mountain its light left them dim;
Others outspeeded it; and others made

'Circles around it, like the clouds that swim
Round the high moon in a bright sea of air;
And more did follow, with exulting hymn,

'The chariot and the captives fettered there:—
But all like bubbles on an eddying flood
Fell into the same track at last, and were

'Borne onward.—I among the multitude
Was swept—me, sweetest flowers delayed not long;
Me, not the shadow nor the solitude;

'Me, not that falling stream's Lethean song;
Me, not the phantom of that early Form
Which moved upon its motion—but among

'The thickest billows of that living storm
I plunged, and bared my bosom to the clime
Of that cold light, whose airs too soon deform.

'Before the chariot had begun to climb
The opposing steep of that mysterious dell,
Behold a wonder worthy of the rhyme

'Of him who from the lowest depths of hell,
Through every paradise and through all glory,
Love led serene, and who returned to tell

'The words of hate and awe; the wondrous story
How all things are transfigured except Love;
For deaf as is a sea, which wrath makes hoary,

'The world can hear not the sweet notes that move
The sphere whose light is melody to lovers—
A wonder worthy of his rhyme.—The grove

'Grew dense with shadows to its inmost covers,
The earth was gray with phantoms, and the air
Was peopled with dim forms, as when there hovers

'A flock of vampire-bats before the glare
Of the tropic sun, bringing, ere evening,
Strange night upon some Indian isle;—thus were

'Phantoms diffused around; and some did fling
Shadows of shadows, yet unlike themselves,
Behind them; some like eaglets on the wing

'Were lost in the white day; others like elves
Danced in a thousand unimagined shapes
Upon the sunny streams and grassy shelves;

'And others sate chattering like restless apes
On vulgar hands, . . .
Some made a cradle of the ermined capes

'Of kingly mantles; some across the tiar
Of pontiffs sate like vultures; others played
Under the crown which girt with empire

'A baby's or an idiot's brow, and made
Their nests in it. The old anatomies
Sate hatching their bare broods under the shade

'Of daemon wings, and laughed from their dead eyes
To reassume the delegated power,
Arrayed in which those worms did monarchize,

'Who made this earth their charnel. Others more
Humble, like falcons, sate upon the fist
Of common men, and round their heads did soar;

'Or like small gnats and flies, as thick as mist
On evening marches, thronged about the brow
Of lawyers, statesmen, priest and theorist;—

'And others, like discoloured flakes of snow
On fairest bosoms and the sunniest hair,
Fell, and were melted by the youthful glow

'Which they extinguished; and like tears they were
A veil to those from whose faint lids they rained
In drops of sorrow. I became aware

'Of whence those forms proceeded which thus stained
The track in which we moved. After brief space,
From every form the beauty slowly waned;

'From every firmest limb and fairest face
The strength and freshness fell like dust, and left
The action and the shape without the grace

'Of life. The marble brow of youth was cleft
With care; and in those eyes where once hope shone,
Desire, like a lioness bereft

'Of her last cub, glared ere it died; each one
Of that great crowd sent forth incessantly
These shadows, numerous as the dead leaves blown

'In autumn evening from a poplar tree.
Each like himself and like each other were
At first; but some distorted seemed to be

'Obscure clouds, moulded by the casual air;
And of this stuff the car's creative ray
Wrought all the busy phantoms that were there,

'As the sun shapes the clouds; thus on the way
Mask after mask fell from the countenance
And form of all; and long before the day

'Was old, the joy which waked like heaven's glance
The sleepers in the oblivious valley, died;
And some grew weary of the ghastly dance,

'And fell, as I have fallen, by the wayside;—
Those soonest from whose forms most shadows passed,
And least of strength and beauty did abide.

'Then, what is life? I cried.'—

Fragment: Rain

The gentleness of rain was in the wind.

# JOHN KEATS

[From] *Epistle to George Keats*

Should he upon an evening ramble fare
With forehead to the soothing breezes bare,
Would he naught see but the dark, silent blue
With all its diamonds trembling through and through?
Or the coy moon, when in the waviness
Of whitest clouds she does her beauty dress,
And staidly paces higher up, and higher,
Like a sweet nun in holy-day attire?

# JOHN KEATS

*Sonnet: Written on the Day that Mr. Leigh Hunt left Prison*

What though, for showing truth to flatter'd state,
   Kind Hunt was shut in prison, yet has he,
   In his immortal spirit, been as free
As the sky-searching lark, and as elate.
Minion of grandeur! think you he did wait?
   Think you he nought but prison walls did see,
   Till, so unwilling, thou unturn'dst the key?
Ah, no! far happier, nobler was his fate!
In Spenser's halls he stray'd, and bowers fair,
   Culling enchanted flowers; and he flew
With daring Milton through the fields of air:
   To regions of his own his genius true
Took happy flights. Who shall his fame impair
   When thou art dead, and all thy wretched crew?

# JOHN KEATS

[From] *Sleep and Poetry*

Could all this be forgotten? Yes, a schism
Nurtured by foppery and barbarism,
Made great Apollo blush for this his land.
Men were thought wise who could not understand
His glories: with a puling infant's force
They sway'd about upon a rocking horse,
And thought it Pegasus. Ah dismal soul'd!
The winds of heaven blew, the ocean roll'd
Its gathering waves—ye felt it not. The blue
Bar'd its eternal bosom, and the dew
Of summer nights collected still to make
The morning precious: beauty was awake!
Why were ye not awake? But ye were dead
To things ye knew not of,—were closely wed
To musty laws lined out with wretched rule
And compass vile: so that ye taught a school
Of dolts to smooth, inlay, and clip, and fit,
Till, like the certain wands of Jacob's wit,
Their verses tallied. Easy was the task:
A thousand handicraftsmen wore the mask
Of Poesy. Ill-fated, impious race!
That blasphem'd the bright Lyrist to his face,
And did not know it,—no, they went about,
Holding a poor, decrepid standard out
Mark'd with most flimsy mottos, and in large
The name of one Boileau!

# JOHN KEATS

[From] Endymion

## Hymn To Pan

"O thou, whose mighty palace roof doth hang
From jagged trunks, and overshadoweth
Eternal whispers, glooms, the birth, life, death
Of unseen flowers in heavy peacefulness;
Who lov'st to see the hamadryads dress
Their ruffled locks where meeting hazels darken;
And through whole solemn hours dost sit, and hearken
The dreary melody of bedded reeds—
In desolate places, where dank moisture breeds
The pipy hemlock to strange overgrowth;
Bethinking thee, how melancholy loth
Thou wast to lose fair Syrinx—do thou now,
By thy love's milky brow!
By all the trembling mazes that she ran,
Hear us, great Pan!

"O thou, for whose soul-soothing quiet, turtles
Passion their voices cooingly 'mong myrtles,
What time thou wanderest at eventide
Through sunny meadows, that outskirt the side
Of thine enmossed realms: O thou, to whom
Broad leaved fig trees even now foredoom
Their ripen'd fruitage; yellow girted bees

Their golden honeycombs; our village leas
Their fairest blossom'd beans and poppied corn;
The chuckling linnet its five young unborn,
To sing for thee; low creeping strawberries
Their summer coolness; pent up butterflies
Their freckled wings; yea, the fresh budding year
All its completions—be quickly near,
By every wind that nods the mountain pine,
O forester divine!

   "Thou, to whom every faun and satyr flies
For willing service; whether to surprise
The squatted hare while in half sleeping fit;
Or upward ragged precipices flit
To save poor lambkins from the eagle's maw;
Or by mysterious enticement draw
Bewildered shepherd to their path again;
Or to tread breathless round the frothy main,
And gather up all fancifullest shells
For thee to tumble into Naiads' cells,
And, being hidden, laugh at their out-peeping;
Or to delight thee with fantastic leaping,
The while they pelt each other on the crown
With silvery oak apples, and fir cones brown—
By all the echoes that about thee ring,
Hear us, O satyr king!

   "O Hearkener to the loud clapping shears,
While ever and anon to his shorn peers
A ram goes bleating: Winder of the horn,
When snouted wild-boars routing tender corn
Anger our huntsmen: breather round our farms,

To keep off mildews, and all weather harms:
Strange ministrant of undescribed sounds,
That come a swooning over hollow grounds,
And wither drearily on barren moors:
Dread opener of the mysterious doors
Leading to universal knowledge—see,
Great son of Dryope,
The many that are come to pay their vows
With leaves about their brows!

"Be still the unimaginable lodge
For solitary thinkings; such as dodge
Conception to the very bourne of heaven,
Then leave the naked brain: be still the leaven,
That spreading in this dull and clodded earth
Gives it a touch ethereal—a new birth:
Be still a symbol of immensity;
A firmament reflected in a sea;
An element filling the space between,
An unknown—but no more: we humbly screen
With uplift hands our foreheads, lowly bending,
And giving out a shout most heaven rending,
Conjure thee to receive our humble Paean,
Upon thy Mount Lycean!"

## Ode to Psyche

O Goddess! hear these tuneless numbers, wrung
  By sweet enforcement and remembrance dear,
And pardon that thy secrets should be sung
  Even in thine own soft-conched ear:
Surely I dreamt to-day, or did I see
  The winged Psyche with awaken'd eyes?
I wander'd in a forest thoughtlessly,
  And, on the sudden, fainting with surprise,
Saw two fair creatures, couched side by side
    In deepest grass, beneath the whisp'ring roof
    Of leaves and trembled blossoms, where there ran
      A brooklet, scarce espy'd:


'Mid hush'd, cool-rooted flowers, fragrant-ey'd,
  Blue, silver-white, and budded Tyrian,
They lay calm-breathing, on the bedded grass;
  Their arms embraced, and their pinions too;
  Their lips touch'd not, but had not bade adieu,
As if disjoined by soft-handed slumber,
And ready still past kisses to outnumber
  At tender eye-dawn of aurorean love:
    The winged boy I knew;
  But who wast thou, O happy, happy dove?
    His Psyche true!

# JOHN KEATS

O latest born and loveliest vision far
   Of all Olympus' faded hierarchy!
Fairer than Phoebe's sapphire-region'd star,
   Or Vesper, amorous glow-worm of the sky;
Fairer than these, though temple thou hast none,
      Nor altar heap'd with flowers;
Nor virgin-choir to make delicious moan
      Upon the midnight hours;
No voice, no lute, no pipe, no incense sweet
   From chain-swung censer teeming;
No shrine, no grove, no oracle, no heat
   Of pale-mouth'd prophet dreaming.

O brightest! though too late for antique vows,
   Too, too late for the fond believing lyre,
When holy were the haunted forest boughs,
   Holy the air, the water, and the fire;
Yet even in these days so far retir'd
   From happy pieties, thy lucent fans,
   Fluttering among the faint Olympians,
I see, and sing, by my own eyes inspir'd.
So let me be thy choir, and make a moan
      Upon the midnight hours;
Thy voice, thy lute, thy pipe, thy incense sweet
   From swinged censer teeming;
Thy shrine, thy grove, thy oracle, thy heat
   Of pale-mouth'd prophet dreaming.

Yes, I will be thy priest, and build a fane
   In some untrodden region of my mind,
Where branched thoughts, new grown with pleasant pa
   Instead of pines shall murmur in the wind:

Far, far around shall those dark-cluster'd trees
  Fledge the wild-ridged mountains steep by steep;
And there by zephyrs, streams, and birds, and bees,
  The moss-lain Dryads shall be lull'd to sleep;
And in the midst of this wide quietness
A rosy sanctuary will I dress
With the wreath'd trellis of a working brain,
  With buds, and bells, and stars without a name,
With all the gardener Fancy e'er could feign,
  Who breeding flowers, will never breed the same:
And there shall be for thee all soft delight
  That shadowy thought can win,
A bright torch, and a casement ope at night,
  To let the warm Love in!

# JOHN KEATS

*Sonnet: To Homer*

Standing aloof in giant ignorance,
  Of thee I hear and of the Cyclades,
As one who sits ashore and longs perchance
  To visit dolphin-coral in deep seas.
So thou wast blind;—but then the veil was rent,
  For Jove uncurtain'd Heaven to let thee live,
And Neptune made for thee a spumy tent,
  And Pan made sing for thee his forest-hive;
Aye on the shores of darkness there is light,
  And precipices show untrodden green,
There is a budding morrow in midnight
  There is a triple sight in blindness keen;
Such seeing hadst thou, as it once befel
  To Dian, Queen of Earth, and Heaven, and Hell.

JOHN KEATS

*Stanzas*

### 1

In a drear-nighted December,
  Too happy, happy tree,
Thy branches ne'er remember
  Their green felicity:
The north cannot undo them,
With a sleety whistle through them,
Nor frozen thawings glue them
  From budding at the prime.

### 2

In a drear-nighted December,
  Too happy, happy brook,
Thy bubblings ne'er remember
  Apollo's summer look;
But with a sweet forgetting,
They stay their crystal fretting,
Never, never petting
  About the frozen time.

### 3

Ah! would 'twere so with many
  A gentle girl and boy
But were there ever any
  Writh'd not at passed joy?
To know the change and feel it
When there is none to heal it,
Nor numbed sense to steal it,
  Was never said in rhyme.

# JOHN KEATS

*Sharing Eve's Apple*

### 1

O blush not so! O blush not so!
  Or I shall think you knowing;
And if you smile the blushing while,
  Then maidenheads are going.

### 2

There's a blush for won't, and a blush for shan't
  And a blush for having done it:
There's a blush for thought and a blush for nought,
  And a blush for just begun it.

### 3

O sigh not so! O sigh not so!
  For it sounds of Eve's sweet pippin;
By these loosen'd lips you have tasted the pips
  And fought in an amorous nipping.

### 4

Will you play once more at nice-cut-core,
  For it only will last our youth out,
And we have the prime of the kissing time,
  We have not one sweet tooth out.

### 5

There's a sigh for yes, and a sigh for no,
  And a sigh for I can't bear it!
O what can be done, shall we stay or run?
  O cut the sweet apple and share it!

# JOHN KEATS

From] Ode to Fanny

Ah! dearest love, sweet home of all my fears,
   And hopes, and joys, and panting miseries,—
To-night, if I may guess, thy beauty wears
      A smile of such delight,
      As brilliant and as bright,
   As when with ravished, aching, vassal eyes,
      Lost in soft amaze,
      I gaze, I gaze!

Who now, with greedy looks, eats up my feast?
   What stare outfaces now my silver moon!
Ah! keep that hand unravished at the least;
      Let, let the amorous burn:—
      But, pr'ythee, do not turn
   The current of your heart from me so soon.
      O! save, in charity,
      The quickest pulse for me.

Save it for me, sweet love! though music breathe
   Voluptuous visions into the warm air,
Though swimming through the dance's dangerous wreath;
      Be like an April day,
      Smiling and cold and gay,
   A temperate lilly, temperate as fair;
      Then, Heaven! there will be
      A warmer June for me.

# JOHN KEATS

Ah! if you prize my subdu'd soul above
    The poor, the fading, brief, pride of an hour;
Let none profane my Holy See of love,
      Or with a rude hand break
      The sacramental cake:
Let none else touch the just new-budded flower;
      If not—may my eyes close,
      Love! on their lost repose.

# JOHN KEATS

From] Lines to Fanny

Where shall I learn to get my peace again?
To banish thoughts of that most hateful land,
Dungeoner of my friends, that wicked strand
Where they were wreck'd and live a wrecked life;
That monstrous region, whose dull rivers pour,
Ever from their sordid urns unto the shore,
Unown'd of any weedy-haired gods;
Whose winds, all zephyrless, hold scourging rods,
Ic'd in the great lakes, to afflict mankind;
Whose rank-grown forests, frosted, black, and blind,
Would fright a Dryad; whose harsh herbag'd meads
Make lean and lank the starv'd ox while he feeds;
There bad flowers have no scent, birds no sweet song,
And great unerring Nature once seems wrong.

O, for some sunny spell
To dissipate the shadows of this hell!
Say they are gone,—with the new dawning light
Steps forth my lady bright!
O, let me once more rest
My soul upon that dazzling breast!
Let once again these aching arms be plac'd,
The tender gaolers of thy waist!
And let me feel that warm breath here and there
To spread a rapture in my very hair,—

# JOHN KEATS

O, the sweetness of the pain!
Give me those lips again!
Enough! Enough! it is enough for me
To dream of thee!

## Lines

Supposed to have been addressed to Fanny Brawne

This living hand, now warm and capable
Of earnest grasping, would, if it were cold
And in the icy silence of the tomb,
So haunt thy days and chill thy dreaming nights
That thou would[st] wish thine own heart dry of blood
So in my veins red life might stream again,
And thou be conscience-calm'd—see here it is
I hold it towards you.

## Ode to a Nightingale

**1**

My heart aches, and a drowsy numbness pains
    My sense, as though of hemlock I had drunk,
Or emptied some dull opiate to the drains
    One minute past, and Lethe-wards had sunk:
'Tis not through envy of thy happy lot,
    But being too happy in thy happiness,—
        That thou, light-winged Dryad of the trees,
            In some melodious plot
    Of beechen green, and shadows numberless,
        Singest of summer in full-throated ease.

**2**

O for a draught of vintage, that hath been
    Cooled a long age in the deep-delved earth,
Tasting of Flora and the country-green,
    Dance, and Provencal song, and sun-burnt mirth!
O for a beaker full of the warm South,
    Full of the true, the blushful Hippocrene,
        With beaded bubbles winking at the brim,
            And purple-stained mouth;
    That I might drink, and leave the world unseen,
        And with thee fade away into the forest dim:

JOHN KEATS

### 3

Fade far away, dissolve, and quite forget
  What thou among the leaves hast never known,
The weariness, the fever, and the fret
  Here, where men sit and hear each other groan;
Where palsy shakes a few, sad, last grey hairs,
  Where youth grows pale, and spectre-thin, and dies;
    Where but to think is to be full of sorrow
      And leaden-eyed despairs;
  Where Beauty cannot keep her lustrous eyes,
    Or new Love pine at them beyond to-morrow.

### 4

Away! Away! for I will fly to thee,
  Not charioted by Bacchus and his pards,
But on the viewless wings of Poesy,
  Though the dull brain perplexes and retards:
Already with thee! tender is the night,
  And haply the Queen-Moon is on her throne,
    Clustered around by all the starry Fays;
      But here there is no light,
  Save what from heaven is with the breezes blown
    Through verdurous glooms and winding mossy way

### 5

I cannot see what flowers are at my feet,
  Nor what soft incense hangs upon the boughs,
But, in embalmed darkness, guess each sweet
  Wherewith the seasonable month endows

The grass, the thicket, and the fruit-tree wild;
   White hawthorn, and the pastoral eglantine;
      Fast-fading violets covered up in leaves;
         And mid-May's eldest child,
   The coming musk-rose, full of dewy wine,
      The murmurous haunt of flies on summer eves.


6

Darkling I listen; and for many a time
   I have been half in love with easeful Death,
Called him soft names in many a mused rhyme,
   To take into the air my quiet breath;
Now more than ever seems it rich to die,
   To cease upon the midnight with no pain,
      While thou art pouring forth thy soul abroad
         In such an ecstasy!
   Still wouldst thou sing, and I have ears in vain—
      To thy high requiem become a sod.


7

Thou wast not borne for death, immortal Bird!
   No hungry generations tread thee down;
The voice I hear this passing night was heard
   In ancient days by emperor and clown:
Perhaps the self-same song that found a path
   Through the sad heart of Ruth, when, sick for home,
      She stood in tears amid the alien corn;
         The same that oft-times hath
   Charmed magic casements, opening on the foam
      Of perilous seas, in faery lands forlorn.

8

Forlorn! the very word is like a bell
  To toll me back from thee to my sole self!
Adieu! the fancy cannot cheat so well
  As she is famed to do, deceiving elf.
Adieu! adieu! thy plaintive anthem fades
    Past the near meadows, over the still stream,
      Up the hill-side; and now 'tis buried deep
        In the next valley-glades:
  Was it a vision, or a waking dream?
    Fled is that music:—do I wake or sleep?

## Ode on a Grecian Urn

### 1

Thou still unravished bride of quietness!
   Thou foster-child of Silence and slow Time,
Sylvan historian, who canst thus express
   A flowery tale more sweetly than our rhyme:
What leaf-fringed legend haunts about thy shape
    Of deities or mortals, or of both
      In Tempe or the dales of Arcady?
    What men or gods are these? What maidens loath?
What mad pursuit? What struggle to escape?
      What pipes and timbrels? What wild ecstasy?

### 2

Heard melodies are sweet, but those unheard
   Are sweeter; therefore, ye soft pipes, play on;
Not to the sensual ear, but, more endeared,
   Pipe to the spirit ditties of no tone:
Fair youth, beneath the trees, thou canst not leave
    Thy song, nor ever can those trees be bare;
      Bold Lover, never, never canst thou kiss,
Though winning near the goal—yet, do not grieve;
      She cannot fade, though thou hast not thy bliss,
    For ever wilt thou love, and she be fair!

### 3

Ah, happy, happy boughs! that cannot shed
   Your leaves, nor ever bid the Spring adieu;
And, happy melodist, unwearied,
   For ever piping songs for ever new;

More happy love! more happy, happy love!
 For ever warm and still to be enjoyed,
  For ever panting and for ever young;
All breathing human passion far above,
 That leaves a heart high sorrowful and cloyed,
  A burning forehead, and a parching tongue.

4

Who are these coming to the sacrifice?
 To what green altar, O mysterious priest,
Lead'st thou that heifer lowing at the skies,
 And all her silken flanks with garlands drest?
What little town by river or sea-shore,
 Or mountain-built with peaceful citadel,
  Is emptied of its folk, this pious morn?
And, little town, thy streets for evermore
 Will silent be; and not a soul to tell
  Why thou art desolate, can e'er return.

5

O Attic shape! Fair attitude! with brede
 Of marble men and maidens overwrought,
With forest branches and the trodden weed;
 Thou silent form! dost tease us out of thought
As doth eternity. Cold Pastoral!
 When old age shall this generation waste,
  Thou shalt remain, in midst of other woe
  Than ours, a friend to man, to whom thou say'st:
'Beauty is truth, truth beauty,—that is all
 Ye know on earth, and all ye need to know.'

*Ode*

Bards of Passion and of Mirth
Ye have left your souls on earth!
Have ye souls in heaven too,
Double-lived in regions new?
Yes, and those of heaven commune
With the spheres of sun and moon;
With the noise of fountains wondrous,
And the parle of voices thunderous:
With the whisper of heaven's trees
And one another, in soft ease
Seated on Elysian lawns
Browsed by none but Dian's fawns;
Underneath large blue-bells tended,
Where the daisies are rose-scented,
And the rose herself has got
Perfume which on earth is not;
Where the nightingale doth sing
Not a senseless, tranced thing,
But divine melodious truth;
Philosophic numbers smooth;
Tales and golden histories
Of heaven and its mysteries.

Thus ye live on high, and then
On the earth ye live again;

And the souls ye left behind you
Teach us, here, the way to find you,
Where your other souls are joying,
Never slumbered, never cloying.
Here, your earth-born souls still speak
The mortals, of their little week;
Of their sorrows and delights;
Of their passions and their spites;
Of their glory and their shame;
What doth strengthen and what maim.
Thus ye teach us every day,
Wisdom, though fled far away.

Bards of Passion and of Mirth,
Ye have left your souls on earth!
Ye have souls in heaven too,
Double-lived in regions new!

*o Autumn*

Season of mists and mellow fruitfulness!
    Close bosom-friend of the maturing sun;
Conspiring with him how to load and bless
    With fruit the vines that round the thatch-eaves run;
To bend with apples the mossed cottage-trees,
    And fill all fruit with ripeness to the core;
      To swell the gourd and plump the hazel shells
    With a sweet kernel; to set budding more,
And still more, later flowers for the bees,
Until they think warm days will never cease,
    For Summer has o'er-brimmed their clammy cells.


Who hath not seen thee oft amid thy store?
    Sometimes whoever seeks abroad may find
Thee sitting careless on a granary floor,
    Thy hair soft-lifted by the winnowing wind;
Or on a half-reaped furrow sound asleep,
    Drowsed with the fume of poppies, while thy hook
      Spares the next swath and all its twined flowers;
And sometime like a gleaner thou dost keep
    Steady thy laden head across a brook;
    Or by a cider-press, with patient look,
      Thou watchest the last oozings, hours by hours.

# JOHN KEATS

Where are the songs of Spring? Ay, where are they?
Think not of them, thou hast thy music too,
While barred clouds bloom the soft-dying day,
And touch the stubble-plains with rosy hue;
Then in a wailful choir the small gnats mourn
Among the river swallows, borne aloft
Or sinking as the light wind lives or dies;
And full-grown lambs loud bleat from hilly bourn;
Hedge-crickets sing; and now with treble soft
The redbreast whistles from a garden-croft,
And gathering swallows twitter in the skies.

## Sonnet: *On First Looking into Chapman's Homer*

Much have I travelled in the realms of gold,
And many goodly states and kingdoms seen;
Round many western islands have I been
Which bards in fealty to Apollo hold.
Oft of one wide expanse had I been told
That deep-browed Homer ruled as his demesne:
Yet did I never breathe its pure serene
Till I heard Chapman speak out loud and bold:
Then felt I like some watcher of the skies
When a new planet swims into his ken;
Or like stout Cortez when with eagle eyes
He stared at the Pacific—and all his men
Looked at each other with a wild surmise—
Silent, upon a peak in Darien.

# JOHN KEATS

*Sonnet: Written in January, 1818*

When I have fears that I may cease to be
Before my pen has gleaned my teeming brain,
Before high piled books, in charact'ry,
Hold like full garners the full-ripened grain;
When I behold, upon the night's starred face,
Huge cloudy symbols of a high romance,
And feel that I may never live to trace
Their shadows, with the magic hand of chance;
And when I feel, fair creature of an hour!
That I shall never look upon thee more,
Never have relish in the faery power
Of unreflecting love!—then on the shore
Of the wide world I stand alone, and think
Till Love and Fame to nothingness do sink.

*Last Sonnet*

Bright star! would I were steadfast as thou art—
Not in lone splendour hung aloft the night,
And watching, with eternal lids apart,
Like Nature's patient sleepless Eremite,
The moving waters at their priestlike task
Of pure ablution round earth's human shores,
Or gazing on the new soft fallen mask
Of snow upon the mountains and the moors.—
No—yet still steadfast, still unchangeable,
Pillowed upon my fair love's ripening breast,
To feel for ever its soft fall and swell,
Awake for ever in a sweet unrest;
Still, still to hear her tender-taken breath,
And so live ever—or else swoon to death.

# JOHN KEATS

*The Eve of St. Agnes*

### I

St. Agnes' Eve—Ah, bitter chill it was!
The owl, for all his feathers, was a-cold;
The hare limp'd trembling through the frozen grass,
And silent was the flock in woolly fold:
Numb were the Beadsman's fingers, while he told
His rosary, and while his frosted breath,
Like pious incense from a censer old,
Seem'd taking flight for heaven, without a death,
Past the sweet Virgin's picture, while his prayer he saith.

### II

His prayer he saith, this patient, holy man;
Then takes his lamp, and riseth from his knees,
And back returneth, meagre, barefoot, wan,
Along the chapel aisle by slow degrees:
The sculptur'd dead, on each side, seem to freeze,
Emprison'd in black, purgatorial rails:
Knights, ladies, praying in dumb orat'ries,
He passeth by; and his weak spirit fails
To think how they may ache in icy hoods and mails.

### III

Northward he turneth through a little door,
And scarce three steps, ere Music's golden tongue
Flatter'd to tears this aged man and poor;
But no—already had his deathbell rung;
The joys of all his life were said and sung:
His was harsh penance on St. Agnes' Eve:
Another way he went, and soon among
Rough ashes sat he for his soul's reprieve,
And all night kept awake, for sinners' sake to grieve.

### IV

That ancient Beadsman heard the prelude soft;
And so it chanc'd, for many a door was wide,
From hurry to and fro. Soon, up aloft,
The silver, snarling trumpets 'gan to chide:
The level chambers, ready with their pride,
Were glowing to receive a thousand guests:
The carved angels, ever eager-ey'd,
Star'd, where upon their heads the cornice rests,
With hair blown back, and wings put cross-wise on their breasts.

### V

At length burst in the argent revelry,
With plume, tiara, and all rich array,
Numerous as shadows haunting faerily
The brain, new stuff'd, in youth, with triumphs gay
Of old romance. These let us wish away,
And turn, sole-thoughted, to one Lady there,
Whose heart had brooded, all that wintry day,
On love, and wing'd St. Agnes' saintly care,
As she had heard old dames full many times declare.

### VI

They told her how, upon St. Agnes' Eve,
Young virgins might have visions of delight,
And soft adorings from their loves receive
Upon the honey'd middle of the night,
If ceremonies due they did aright;
As, supperless to bed they must retire,
And couch supine their beauties, lilly white;
Nor look behind, nor sideways, but require
Of Heaven with upward eyes for all that they desire.

### VII

Full of this whim was thoughtful Madeline:
The music, yearning like a God in pain,
She scarcely heard: her maiden eyes divine,
Fix'd on the floor, saw many a sweeping train
Pass by—she heeded not at all: in vain
Came many a tiptoe, amorous cavalier,
And back retir'd; not cool'd by high disdain,
But she saw not: her heart was otherwhere:
She sigh'd for Agnes' dreams, the sweetest of the year.

### VIII

She danc'd along with vague, regardless eyes,
Anxious her lips, her breathing quick and short:
The hallow'd hour was near at hand: she sighs
Amid the timbrels, and the throng'd resort
Of whisperers in anger, or in sport;
'Mid looks of love, defiance, hate, and scorn,
Hoodwink'd with faery fancy; all amort,
Save to St. Agnes and her lambs unshorn,
And all the bliss to be before to-morrow morn.

### IX

So, purposing each moment to retire,
She linger'd still. Meantime, across the moors,
Had come young Porphyro, with heart on fire
For Madeline. Beside the portal doors,
Buttress'd from moonlight, stands he, and implores
All saints to give him sight of Madeline,
But for one moment in the tedious hours,
That he might gaze and worship all unseen;
Perchance speak, kneel, touch, kiss—in sooth such things have
    been.

### X

He ventures in: let no buzz'd whisper tell:
All eyes be muffled, or a hundred swords
Will storm his heart, Love's fev'rous citadel:
For him, these chambers held barbarian hordes,
Hyena foemen, and hot-blooded lords,
Whose very dogs would execrations howl
Against his lineage: not one breast affords
Him any mercy, in that mansion foul,
Save one old beldame, weak in body and in soul.

### XI

Ah, happy chance! the aged creature came,
Shuffling along with ivory-headed wand,
To where he stood, hid from the torch's flame,
Behind a broad hall-pillar, far beyond
The sound of merriment and chorus bland:
He startled her; but soon she knew his face,
And grasp'd his fingers in her palsied hand,
Saying, "Mercy, Porphyro! hie thee from this place;
"They are all here to-night, the whole blood-thirsty race!

### XII

"Get hence! get hence! there's dwarfish Hildebrand;
"He had a fever late, and in the fit
"He cursed thee and thine, both house and land:
"Then there's that old Lord Maurice, not a whit
"More tame for his grey hairs—Alas me! flit!
"Flit like a ghost away."—"Ah, Gossip dear,
"We're safe enough; here in this arm-chair sit,
"And tell me how."—"Good Saints! not here, not here;
"Follow me, child, or else these stones will be thy bier."

### XIII

He follow'd through a lowly arched way,
Brushing the cobwebs with his lofty plume,
And as she mutter'd "Well-a—well-a-day!"
He found him in a little moonlight room,
Pale, lattic'd, chill, and silent as a tomb.
"Now tell me where is Madeline," said he,
"O tell me, Angela, by the holy loom
"Which none but secret sisterhood may see,
"When they St. Agnes' wool are weaving piously."

### XIV

"St. Agnes! Ah! it is St. Agnes' Eve—
"Yet men will murder upon holy days:
"Thou must hold water in a witch's sieve,
"And be liege-lord of all the Elves and Fays,
"To venture so: it fills me with amaze
"To see thee, Porphyro!—St. Agnes' Eve!
"God's help! my lady fair the conjuror plays
"This very night: good angels her deceive!
"But let me laugh awhile, I've mickle time to grieve."

### XV

Feebly she laugheth in the languid moon,
While Porphyro upon her face doth look,
Like puzzled urchin on an aged crone
Who keepeth clos'd a wond'rous riddle-book,
As spectacled she sits in chimney nook.
But soon his eyes grew brilliant, when she told
His lady's purpose; and he scarce could brook
Tears, at the thought of those enchantments cold,
And Madeline asleep in lap of legends old.

### XVI

Sudden a thought came like a full-blown rose,
Flushing his brow, and in his pained heart
Made purple riot: then doth he propose
A stratagem, that makes the beldame start:
"A cruel man and impious thou art:
"Sweet lady, let her pray, and sleep, and dream
"Alone with her good angels, far apart
"From wicked men like thee. Go, go!—I deem
"Thou canst not surely be the same that thou didst seem."

### XVII

"I will not harm her, by all saints I swear,"
Quoth Porphyro: "O may I ne'er find grace
"When my weak voice shall whisper its last prayer,
"If one of her soft ringlets I displace,
"Or look with ruffian passion in her face:
"Good Angela, believe me by these tears;
"Or I will, even in a moment's space,
"Awake, with horrid shout, my foemen's ears,
"And beard them, though they be more fang'd than wolves and
    bears."

## XVIII

"Ah! why wilt thou affright a feeble soul?
"A poor, weak, palsy-stricken, churchyard thing,
"Whose passing-bell may ere the midnight toll;
"Whose prayers for thee, each morn and evening,
"Were never miss'd."—Thus planning, doth she bring
A gentler speech from burning Porphyro;
So woeful, and of such deep sorrowing,
That Angela gives promise she will do
Whatever he shall wish, betide her weal or woe.

## XIX

Which was, to lead him, in close secrecy,
Even to Madeline's chamber, and there hide
Him in a closet, of such privacy
That he might see her beauty unespy'd,
And win perhaps that night a peerless bride,
While legion'd faeries pac'd the coverlet,
And pale enchantment held her sleepy-ey'd.
Never on a such a night have lovers met,
Since Merlin paid his Demon all the monstrous debt.

## XX

"It shall be as thou wishest," said the Dame:
"All cates and dainties shall be stored there
"Quickly on this feast-night: by the tambour frame
"Her own lute thou wilt see: no time to spare,
"For I am slow and feeble, and scarce dare
"On such a catering trust my dizzy head.
"Wait here, my child, with patience; kneel in prayer
"The while: Ah! thou must needs the lady wed,
"Or may I never leave my grave among the dead."

### XXI

So saying, she hobbled off with busy fear.
The lover's endless minutes slowly pass'd;
The dame return'd, and whisper'd in his ear
To follow her; with aged eyes aghast
From fright of dim espial. Safe at last,
Through many a dusky gallery, they gain
The maiden's chamber, silken, hush'd, and chaste;
Where Porphyro took covert, pleas'd amain.
His poor guide hurried back with agues in her brain.

### XXII

Her falt'ring hand upon the balustrade,
Old Angela was feeling for the stair,
When Madeline, St. Agnes' charmed maid,
Rose, like a mission'd spirit, unaware:
With silver taper's light, and pious care,
She turn'd, and down the aged gossip led
To a safe level matting. Now prepare,
Young Porphyro, for gazing on that bed;
She comes, she comes again, like ring-dove fray'd and fled.

### XXIII

Out went the taper as she hurried in;
Its little smoke, in pallid moonshine, died:
She clos'd the door, she panted, all akin
To spirits of the air, and visions wide:
No uttered syllable, or, woe betide!
But to her heart, her heart was voluble,
Paining with eloquence her balmy side;
As though a tongueless nightingale should swell
Her throat in vain, and die, heart-stifled, in her dell.

JOHN KEATS

## XXIV

A casement high and triple-arch'd there was,
All garlanded with carven imag'ries
Of fruits, and flowers, and bunches of knot-grass,
And diamonded with panes of quaint device,
Innumerable of stains and splendid dyes,
As are the tiger-moth's deep-damask'd wings;
And in the midst, 'mong thousand heraldries,
And twilight saints, and dim emblazonings,
A shielded scutcheon blush'd with blood of queens and kings.

## XXV

Full on this casement shone the wintry moon,
And threw warm gules on Madeline's fair breast,
As down she knelt for heaven's grace and boon;
Rose-bloom fell on her hands, together prest,
And on her silver cross soft amethyst,
And on her hair a glory, like a saint:
She seem'd a splendid angel, newly drest,
Save wings, for heaven:—Porphyro grew faint:
She knelt, so pure a thing, so free from mortal taint.

## XXVI

Anon his heart revives: her vespers done,
Of all its wreathed pearls her hair she frees;
Unclasps her warmed jewels one by one;
Loosens her fragrant bodice; by degrees
Her rich attire creeps rustling to her knees:
Half-hidden, like a mermaid in sea-weed,
Pensive awhile she dreams awake, and sees,
In fancy, fair St. Agnes in her bed,
But dares not look behind, or all the charm is fled.

## XXVII

Soon, trembling in her soft and chilly nest,
In sort of wakeful swoon, perplex'd she lay,
Until the poppied warmth of sleep oppress'd
Her soothed limbs, and soul fatigued away;
Flown, like a thought, until the morrow-day;
Blissfully haven'd both from joy and pain;
Clasp'd like a missal where swart Paynims pray;
Blinded alike from sunshine and from rain,
As though a rose should shut, and be a bud again.

## XXVIII

Stol'n to this paradise, and so entranced,
Porphyro gaz'd upon her empty dress,
And listen'd to her breathing, if it chanced
To wake into a slumberous tenderness;
Which when he heard, that minute did he bless,
And breath'd himself: then from the closet crept,
Noiseless as fear in a wide wilderness,
And over the hush'd carpet, silent, stept,
And 'tween the curtains peep'd, where, lo!—how fast she slept.

## XXIX

Then by the bed-side, where the faded moon
Made a dim, silver twilight, soft he set
A table, and, half anguish'd, threw thereon
A cloth of woven crimson, gold, and jet:—
O for some drowsy Morphean amulet!
The boisterous, midnight, festive clarion,
The kettle-drum, and far-heard clarionet,
Affray his ears, though but in dying tone:—
The hall door shuts again, and all the noise is gone.

# JOHN KEATS

## XXX

And still she slept an azure-lidded sleep,
In blanched linen, smooth, and lavender'd,
While he from forth the closet brought a heap.
Of candied apple, quince, and plum, and gourd;
With jellies soother than the creamy curd,
And lucent syrops, tinct with cinnamon;
Manna and dates, in argosy transferr'd
From Fez; and spiced dainties, every one,
From silken Samarcand to cedar'd Lebanon.

## XXXI

These delicates he heap'd with glowing hand
On golden dishes and in baskets bright
Of wreathed silver: sumptuous they stand
In the retired quiet of the night,
Filling the chilly room with perfume light.—
"And now, my love, my seraph fair, awake!
"Thou art my heaven, and I thine eremite:
"Open thine eyes, for meek St. Agnes' sake,
"Or I shall drowse beside thee, so my soul doth ache."

## XXXII

Thus whispering, his warm, unnerved arm
Sank in her pillow. Shaded was her dream
By the dusk curtains:—'Twas a midnight charm
Impossible to melt as iced stream:
The lustrous salvers in the moonlight gleam;
Broad golden fringe upon the carpet lies:
It seem'd he never, never could redeem
From such a steadfast spell his lady's eyes;
So mus'd awhile, entoil'd in woofed phantasies.

### XXXIII

Awakening up, he took her hollow lute,—
Tumultuous,—and, in chords that tenderest be,
He play'd an ancient ditty, long since mute,
In Provence call'd, "La belle dame sans mercy:"
Close to her ear touching the melody;—
Wherewith disturb'd, she utter'd a soft moan:
He ceas'd—she panted quick—and suddenly
Her blue affrayed eyes wide open shone:
Upon his knees he sank, pale as smooth-sculptured stone.

### XXXIV

Her eyes were open, but she still beheld,
Now wide awake, the vision of her sleep:
There was a painful change, that nigh expell'd
The blisses of her dream so pure and deep,
At which fair Madeline began to weep,
And moan forth witless words with many a sigh;
While still her gaze on Porphyro would keep;
Who knelt, with joined hands and piteous eye,
Fearing to move or speak, she look'd so dreamingly.

### XXXV

"Ah, Porphyro!" said she, "but even now
"Thy voice was at sweet tremble in mine ear,
"Made tuneable with every sweetest vow;
"And those sad eyes were spiritual and clear:
"How chang'd thou art! how pallid, chill, and drear!
"Give me that voice again, my Porphyro,
"Those looks immortal, those complainings dear!
"Oh leave me not in this eternal woe,
"For if thou diest, my Love, I know not where to go."

### XXXVI

Beyond a mortal man impassion'd far
At these voluptuous accents, he arose,
Ethereal, flush'd, and like a throbbing star
Seen mid the sapphire heaven's deep repose;
Into her dream he melted, as the rose
Blendeth its odour with the violet,—
Solution sweet: meantime the frost-wind blows
Like Love's alarum pattering the sharp sleet
Against the window-panes; St. Agnes' moon hath set.

### XXXVII

'Tis dark: quick pattereth the flaw-blown sleet:
"This is no dream, my bride, my Madeline!"
'Tis dark: the iced gusts still rave and beat:
"No dream, alas! alas! and woe is mine!
"Porphyro will leave me here to fade and pine,—
"Cruel! what traitor could thee hither bring?
"I curse not, for my heart is lost in thine,
"Though thou forsakest a deceived thing;—
"A dove forlorn and lost with sick unpruned wing."

### XXXVIII

"My Madeline! sweet dreamer! lovely bride!
"Say, may I be for aye thy vassal blest?
"Thy beauty's shield, heart-shap'd and vermeil dy'd?
"Ah, silver shrine, here will I take my rest
"After so many hours of toil and quest,
"A famish'd pilgrim,—sav'd by miracle.
"Though I have found, I will not rob thy nest
"Saving of thy sweet self; if thou think'st well
"To trust, fair Madeline, to no rude infidel.

### XXXIX

"Hark! 'tis an elfin-storm from faery land,
"Of haggard seeming, but a boon indeed:
"Arise—arise! the morning is at hand;—
"The bloated wassaillers will never heed;—
"Let us away, my love, with happy speed;
"There are no ears to hear, or eyes to see,—
"Drown'd all in Rhenish and the sleepy mead:
"Awake! arise! my love, and fearless be,
"For o'er the southern moors I have a home for thee."

### XL

She hurried at his words, beset with fears,
For there were sleeping dragons all around,
At glaring watch, perhaps, with ready spears—
Down the wide stairs a darkling way they found.—
In all the house was heard no human sound.
A chain-droop'd lamp was flickering by each door;
The arras, rich with horseman, hawk, and hound,
Flutter'd in the besieging wind's uproar;
And the long carpets rose along the gusty floor.

### XLI

They glide, like phantoms, into the wide hall;
Like phantoms, to the iron porch, they glide;
Where lay the Porter, in uneasy sprawl,
With a huge empty flaggon by his side:
The wakeful bloodhound rose, and shook his hide,
But his sagacious eye an inmate owns:
By one, and one, the bolts full easy slide:—
The chains lie silent on the footworn stones;—
The key turns, and the door upon its hinges groans.

# JOHN KEATS

## XLII

And they are gone: aye, ages long ago
These lovers fled away into the storm.
That night the Baron dreamt of many a woe,
And all his warrior-guests, with shade and form
Of witch, and demon, and large coffin-worm,
Were long be-nightmar'd. Angela the old
Died palsy-twitch'd, with meagre face deform;
The Beadsman, after thousand aves told,
For aye unsought for slept among his ashes cold.

# JOHN KEATS

[From] *Hyperion*

## Book I

Deep in the shady sadness of a vale
Far sunken from the healthy breath of morn,
Far from the fiery noon, and eve's one star,
Sat gray-hair'd Saturn, quiet as a stone,
Still as the silence round about his lair;
Forest on forest hung about his head
Like cloud on cloud. No stir of air was there,
Not so much life as on a summer's day
Robs not one light seed from the feather's grass,
But where the dead leaf fell, there did it rest.
A stream went voiceless by, still deadened more
By reason of his fallen divinity
Spreading a shade: the Naiad 'mid her reeds
Press'd her cold finger closer to her lips.

Along the margin-sand large foot-marks went,
No further than to where his feet had stray'd,
And slept there since. Upon the sodden ground
His old right hand lay nerveless, listless, dead,
Unsceptred; and his realmless eyes were closed;
While his bow'd head seem'd list'ning to the Earth,
His ancient mother, for some comfort yet.

# JOHN KEATS

It seem'd no force could wake him from his place;
But there came one, who with a kindred hand
Touch'd his wide shoulders, after bending low
With reverence, though to one who knew it not.
She was a Goddess of the infant world;
By her in stature the tall Amazon
Had stood a pigmy's height: she would have ta'en
Achilles by the hair and bent his neck;
Or with a finger stay'd Ixion's wheel.
Her face was large as that of Memphian sphinx,
Pedestal'd haply in a palace court,
When sages look'd to Egypt for their lore.
But oh! how unlike marble was that face:
How beautiful, if sorrow had not made
Sorrow more beautiful than Beauty's self.
There was a listening fear in her regard,
As if calamity had but begun;
As if the vanward clouds of evil days
Had spent their malice, and the sullen rear
Was with its stored thunder labouring up.
One hand she press'd upon that aching spot
Where beats the human heart, as if just there,
Though an immortal, she felt cruel pain:
The other upon Saturn's bended neck
She laid, and to the level of his ear
Leaning with parted lips, some words she spake
In solemn tenour and deep organ tone:
Some mourning words, which in our feeble tongue
Would come in these like accents; O how frail
To that large utterance of the early Gods!
"Saturn, look up!—though wherefore, poor old King?

"I have no comfort for thee, no not one:
"I cannot say, 'O wherefore sleepest thou?'
"For heaven is parted from thee, and the earth
"Knows thee not, thus afflicted, for a God;
"And ocean too, with all its solemn noise,
"Has from thy sceptre pass'd; and all the air
"Is emptied of thine hoary majesty.
"Thy thunder, conscious of the new command,
"Rumbles reluctant o'er our fallen house;
"And thy sharp lightning in unpractis'd hands
"Scorches and burns our once serene domain.
"O aching time! O moments big as years!
"All as ye pass swell out the monstrous truth,
"And press it so upon our weary griefs
"That unbelief has not a space to breathe.
"Saturn, sleep on:—O thoughtless, why did I
"Thus violate thy slumbrous solitude?
"Why should I ope thy melancholy eyes?
"Saturn, sleep on! while at thy feet I weep."

   As when, upon a tranced summer-night,
Those green-rob'd senators of mighty woods,
Tall oaks, branch-charmed by the earnest stars,
Dream, and so dream all night without a stir,
Save from one gradual solitary gust
Which comes upon the silence, and dies off,
As if the ebbing air had but one wave;
So came these words and went; the while in tears
She touch'd her fair large forehead to the ground,
Just where her falling hair might be outspread
A soft and silken mat for Saturn's feet.

# JOHN KEATS

One moon, with alteration slow, had shed
Her silver seasons four upon the night,
And still these two were postured motionless,
Like natural sculpture in cathedral cavern;
The frozen God still couchant on the earth,
And the sad Goddess weeping at his feet:
Until at length old Saturn lifted up
His faded eyes, and saw his kingdom gone,
And all the gloom and sorrow of the place,
And that fair kneeling Goddess; and then spake,
As with a palsied tongue, and while his beard
Shook horrid with such aspen-malady:
"O tender spouse of gold Hyperion,
"Thea, I feel thee ere I see thy face;
"Look up, and let me see our doom in it;
"Look up, and tell me if this feeble shape
"Is Saturn's; tell me, if thou hear'st the voice
"Of Saturn; tell me, if this wrinkling brow,
"Naked and bare of its great diadem,
"Peers like the front of Saturn. Who had power
"To make me desolate? whence came the strength?
"How was it nurtur'd to such bursting forth,
"While Fate seem'd strangled in my nervous grasp?
"But it is so; and I am smother'd up,
"And buried from all godlike exercise
"Of influence benign on planets pale,
"Of admonitions to the winds and seas,
"Of peaceful sway above man's harvesting,
"And all those acts which Deity supreme
"Doth ease its heart of love in.—I am gone
"Away from my own bosom: I have left

"My strong identity, my real self,
"Somewhere between the throne, and where I sit
"Here on this spot of earth. Search, Thea, search!
"Open thy eyes eterne, and sphere them round
"Upon all space: space starr'd, and lorn of light;
"Space region'd with life-air; and barren void;
"Spaces of fire, and all the yawn of hell.—
"Search, Thea, search! and tell me, if thou seest
"A certain shape or shadow, making way
"With wings or chariot fierce to repossess
"A heaven he lost erewhile: it must—it must
"Be of ripe progress—Saturn must be King.
"Yes, there must be a golden victory;
"There must be Gods thrown down, and trumpets blown
"Of triumph calm, and hymns of festival
"Upon the gold clouds metropolitan,
"Voices of soft proclaim, and silver stir
"Of strings in hollow shells; and there shall be
"Beautiful things made new, for the surprise
"Of the sky-children; I will give command:
"Thea! Thea! Thea! where is Saturn?"

    This passion lifted him upon his feet,
And made his hands to struggle in the air,
His Druid locks to shake and ooze with sweat,
His eyes to fever out, his voice to cease.
He stood, and heard not Thea's sobbing deep;
A little time, and then again he snatch'd
Utterance thus.—"But cannot I create?
"Cannot I form? Cannot I fashion forth
"Another world, another universe,

"To overbear and crumble this to nought?
"Where is another chaos? Where?"—That word
Found way unto Olympus, and made quake
The rebel three.—Thea was startled up,
And in her bearing was a sort of hope,
As thus she quick-voiced spake, yet full of awe.

   "This cheers our fallen house: come to our friends,
"O Saturn! come away, and give them heart;
"I know the covert, for thence came I hither."
Thus brief; then with beseeching eyes she went
With backward footing through the shade a space:
He follow'd, and she turn'd to lead the way
Through aged boughs, that yielded like the mist
Which eagles cleave upmounting from their nest.

   Meanwhile in other realms big tears were shed,
More sorrow like to this, and such like woe,
Too huge for mortal tongue or pen of scribe:
The Titans fierce, self-hid, or prison-bound,
Groan'd for the old allegiance once more
And listen'd in sharp pain for Saturn's voice.
But one of the whole mammoth-brood still kept
His sov'reignty, and rule, and majesty;—
Blazing Hyperion on his orbed fire
Still sat, still snuff'd the incense, teeming up
From man to the sun's God; yet unsecure:
For as among us mortals omens drear
Fright and perplex, so also shuddered he—
Not at dog's howl, or gloom-bird's hated screech,
Or the familiar visiting of one

Upon the first toll of his passing-bell,
Or prophesyings of the midnight lamp;
But horrors, portion'd to a giant nerve,
Oft made Hyperion ache. His palace bright
Bastion'd with pyramids of glowing gold,
And touch'd with shade of bronzed obelisks,
Glar'd a blood-red through all its thousand courts,
Arches, and domes, and fiery galleries;
And all its curtains of Aurorian clouds
Flush'd angerly: while sometimes eagle's wings,
Unseen before by Gods or wondering men,
Darken'd the place; and neighing steeds were heard,
Not heard before by Gods or wondering men.
Also, when he would taste the spicy wreaths
Of incense, breath'd aloft from sacred hills,
Instead of sweets, his ample palate took
Savour of poisonous brass and metal sick:
And so, when harbour'd in the sleepy west,
After the full completion of fair day,—
For rest divine upon exalted couch
And slumber in the arms of melody,
He pac'd away the pleasant hours of ease
With stride colossal, on from hall to hall;
While far within each aisle and deep recess,
His winged minions in close clusters stood,
Amaz'd and full of fear; like anxious men
Who on wide plains gather in panting troops,
When earthquakes jar their battlements and towers.
Even now, while Saturn, rous'd from icy trance,
Went step for step with Thea through the woods,
Hyperion, leaving twilight in the rear,

Came slope upon the threshold of the west;
Then, as was wont, his palace-door flew ope
In smoothest silence, save what solemn tubes,
Blown by the serious Zephyrs, gave of sweet
And wandering sounds, slow-breathed melodies;
And like a rose in vermeil tint and shape,
In fragrance soft, and coolness to the eye,
That inlet to severe magnificence
Stood full blown, for the God to enter in.

He enter'd, but he enter'd full of wrath;
His flaming robes stream'd out beyond his heels,
And gave a roar, as if of earthly fire,
That scar'd away the meek ethereal Hours
And made their dove-wings tremble. On he flared,
From stately nave to nave, from vault to vault,
Through bowers of fragrant and enwreathed light,
And diamond-paved lustrous long arcades,
Until he reach'd the great main cupola;
There standing fierce beneath, he stampt his foot,
And from the basements deep to the high towers
Jarr'd his own golden region; and before
The quavering thunder thereupon had ceas'd,
His voice leapt out, despite of godlike curb,
To this result: "O dreams of day and night!
"O monstrous forms! O effigies of pain!
"O spectres busy in a cold, cold gloom!
"O lank-ear'd Phantoms of black-weeded pools!
"Why do I know ye? why have I seen ye? why
"Is my eternal essence thus distraught
"To see and to behold these horrors new?

"Saturn is fallen, am I too to fall?
"Am I to leave this haven of my rest,
"This cradle of my glory, this soft clime,
"This calm luxuriance of blissful light,
"These crystalline pavilions, and pure fanes,
"Of all my lucent empire? It is left
"Deserted, void, nor any haunt of mine.
"The blaze, the splendor, and the symmetry,
"I cannot see—but darkness, death and darkness.
"Even here, into my centre of repose,
"The shady visions come to domineer,
"Insult, and blind, and stifle up my pomp.—
"Fall!—No, by Tellus and her briny robes!
"Over the fiery frontier of my realms
"I will advance a terrible right arm
"Shall scare that infant thunderer, rebel Jove,
"And bid old Saturn take his throne again."—
He spake, and ceas'd, the while a heavier threat
Held struggle with his throat but came not forth;
For as in theatres of crowded men
Hubbub increases more they call out "Hush!"
So at Hyperion's words the phantoms pale
Bestirr'd themselves, thrice horrible and cold;
And from the mirror'd level where he stood
A mist arose, as from a scummy marsh.
At this, through all his bulk an agony
Crept gradual, from the feet unto the crown,
Like a lithe serpent vast and muscular
Making slow way, with head and neck convuls'd
From over-strained might. Releas'd, he fled
To the eastern gates, and full six dewy hours

Before the dawn in season due should blush,
He breath'd fierce breath against the sleepy portals,
Clear'd them of heavy vapours, burst them wide
Suddenly on the ocean's chilly streams.
The planet orb of fire, whereon he rode
Each day from east to west the heavens through,
Spun round in sable curtaining of clouds;
Not therefore veiled quite, blindfold, and hid,
But ever and anon the glancing spheres,
Circles, and arcs, and broad-belting colure,
Glow'd through, and wrought upon the muffling dark
Sweet-shaped lightnings from the nadir deep
Up to the zenith,—hieroglyphics old,
Which sages and keen-ey'd astrologers
Then living on the earth, with labouring thought
Won from the gaze of many centuries:
Now lost, save what we find on remnants huge
Of stone, or marble swart; their import gone,
Their wisdom long since fled. —Two wings this orb
Possess'd for glory, two fair argent wings,
Ever exalted at the God's approach:
And now, from forth the gloom their plumes immense
Rose, one by one, till all outspreaded were;
While still the dazzling globe maintain'd eclipse,
Awaiting for Hyperion's command.
Fain would he have commanded, fain took throne
And bid the day begin, if but for change.
He might not:—No, though a primeval God:
The sacred seasons might not be disturb'd.
Therefore the operations of the dawn
Stay'd in their birth, even as here 'tis told.

Those silver wings expanded sisterly,
Eager to sail their orb; the porches wide
Open'd upon the dusk demesnes of night;
And the bright Titan, phrenzied with new woes,
Unus'd to bend, by hard compulsion bent
His spirit to the sorrow of the time;
And all along a dismal rack of clouds,
Upon the boundaries of day and night,
He stretch'd himself in grief and radiance faint.
There as he lay, the Heaven with its stars
Look'd down on him with pity, and the voice
Of Coelus, from the universal space,
Thus whisper'd low and solemn in his ear.
"O brightest of my children dear, earth-born
"And sky-engendered, Son of Mysteries
"All unrevealed even to the powers
"Which met at thy creating; at whose joys
"And palpitations sweet, and pleasures soft,
"I, Coelus, wonder, how they came and whence;
"And at the fruits thereof what shapes they be,
"Distinct, and visible; symbols divine,
"Manifestations of that beauteous life
"Diffus'd unseen throughout eternal space:
"Of these new-form'd art thou, oh brightest child!
"Of these, thy brethren and the Goddesses!
"There is sad feud among ye, and rebellion
"Of son against his sire. I saw him fall,
"I saw my first-born tumbled from his throne!
"To me his arms were spread, to me his voice
"Found way from forth the thunders round his head!
"Pale wox I, and in vapours hid my face.

JOHN KEATS

"Art thou, too, near such doom? vague fear there is:
"For I have seen my sons most unlike Gods.
"Divine ye were created, and divine
"In sad demeanour, solemn, undisturb'd,
"Unruffled, like high Gods, ye liv'd and ruled:
"Now I behold in you fear, hope, and wrath;
"Actions of rage and passion; even as
"I see them, on the mortal world beneath,
"In men who die. —This is the grief, O Son!
"Sad sign of ruin, sudden dismay, and fall!
"Yet do thou strive; as thou art capable,
"As thou canst move about, an evident God;
"And canst oppose to each malignant hour
"Ethereal presence:—I am but a voice;
"My life is but the life of winds and tides,
"No more than winds and tides can I avail:—
"But thou canst. —Be thou therefore in the van
"Of circumstance; yea, seize the arrow's barb
"Before the tense string murmur. —To the earth!
"For there thou wilt find Saturn, and his woes.
"Meantime I will keep watch on thy bright sun,
"And of thy seasons be a careful nurse."—
Ere half this region-whisper had come down,
Hyperion arose, and on the stars
Lifted his curved lids, and kept them wide
Until it ceas'd; and still he kept them wide:
And still they were the same bright, patient stars.
Then with a slow incline of his broad breast,
Like to a diver in the pearly seas,
Forward he stoop'd over the airy shore,
And plung'd all noiseless into the deep night.

# GEORGE DARLEY

[From] *Nepenthe*

### O Blest Unfabled Incense Tree

O blest unfabled Incense Tree,
That burns in glorious Araby,
With red scent chalicing the air,
Till earth-life grow Elysian there!

Half-buried to her flaming breast
In this bright tree, she makes her nest,
Hundred-sunned Phoenix! when she must
Crumble at length to hoary dust!

Her gorgeous death-bed! her rich pyre
Burnt up with aromatic fire!
Her urn, sight high from spoiler men!
Her birthplace when self-born again!

The mountainless green wilds among,
Here ends she her unechoing song!
With amber tears and odorous sighs
Mourned by the desert where she dies!

# GEORGE DARLEY

O, fast her amber blood doth flow
   From the heart-wounded Incense Tree,
Fast as earth's deep-embosomed woe
   In silent rivulets to the sea!

Beauty may weep her fair first-born,
   Perchance in as resplendent tears,
Such golden dewdrops bow like corn
   When the stern sickleman appears.

But oh! such perfume to a bower
   Never allured sweet-seeking bee,
As to sip fast that nectarous shower
   A thirstier minstrel drew in me!

# THOMAS LOVELL BEDDOES

*Song*

A ho! A ho!
Love's horn doth blow,
And he will out a-hawking go.
His shafts are light as beauty's sighs,
And bright as midnight's brightest eyes,
And round his starry way
The swan-winged horses of the skies,
With summer's music in their manes,
Curve their fair necks to zephyr's reins,
And urge their graceful play.

A ho! A ho!
Love's horn doth blow,
And he will out a-hawking go.
The sparrows flutter round his wrist,
The feathery thieves that Venus kissed
And taught their morning song;
The linnets seek the airy list,
And swallows too, small pets of Spring,
Beat back the gale with swifter wing,
And dart and wheel along.

A ho! A ho!
Love's horn doth blow,
And he will out a-hawking go.

# THOMAS LOVELL BEDDOES

Now woe to every gnat that skips
To filch the fruit of ladies' lips,
His felon blood is shed;
And woe to flies, whose airy ships
On beauty cast their anchoring bite,
And bandit wasp, that naughty wight,
Whose sting is slaughter-red.

# THOMAS LOVELL BEDDOES

## Song

By female voices

We have bathed, where none have seen us,
   In the lake and the fountain,
      Underneath the charmèd statue
Of the timid, bending Venus,
   When the water-nymphs were counting
In the waves the stars of night,
      And those maidens started at you,
Your limbs shone through so soft and bright,
      But no secrets dare we tell,
         For thy slaves unlace thee,
         And he, who shall embrace thee,
      Waits to try thy beauty's spell.

By male voices

We have crowned the queen of women,
   Since love's love, the rose, hath kept her
      Court within thy lips and blushes,
And thine eye, in beauty swimming,
   Kissing, we rendered up the sceptre,
At whose touch the startled soul
      Like an ocean bounds and gushes,
And spirits bend at thy control.
      But no secrets dare we tell,
         For thy slaves unlace thee,
         And he, who shall embrace thee,
      Is at hand, and so farewell.

# THOMAS LOVELL BEDDOES

*Song*

Old Adam, the carrion crow,
  The old crow of Cairo;
He sat in the shower, and let it flow
  Under his tail and over his crest;
    And through every feather
    Leaked the wet weather;
  And the bough swung under his nest;
  For his beak it was heavy with marrow.
    Is that the wind dying? O no;
    It's only two devils, that blow
    Through a murderer's bones, to and fro,
      In the ghost's moonshine.

Ho! Eve, my grey carrion wife,
  When we have supped on king's marrow,
Where shall we drink and make merry our life?
  Our nest it is queen Cleopatra's skull,
    'Tis cloven and cracked,
    And battered and hacked,
  But with tears of blue eyes it is full:
  Let us drink then, my raven of Cairo.
    Is that the wind dying? O no;
    It's only two devils, that blow
    Through a murderer's bones, to and fro,
      In the ghost's moonshine.

# THOMAS LOVELL BEDDOES

*A Beautiful Night*

How lovely is the heaven of this night,
How deadly still is earth! The forest brute
Has crept into his cave, and laid himself
Where sleep has made him harmless like the lamb.
The horrid snake, his venom now forgot,
Is still and innocent as the honied flower
Under his head: and man, in whom are met
Leopard and snake, and all the gentleness
And beauty of the young lamb and the bud,
Has let his ghost out, put his thoughts aside
And lent his senses unto death himself.

# THOMAS LOVELL BEDDOES

Man's Anxious, but Ineffectual Guard Against Death

Luckless man
Avoids the miserable bodkin's point,
And, flinching from the insect's little sting,
In pitiful security keeps watch,
While 'twixt him and that hypocrite the sun,
To which he prays, comes windless pestilence,
Transparent as a glass of poisoned water
Through which the drinker sees his murderer smiling;
She stirs no dust, and makes no grass to nod,
Yet every footstep is a thousand graves,
And every breath of her's as full of ghosts
As a sunbeam with motes.

# ALFRED TENNYSON

## Mariana

With blackest moss the flower-plots
   Were thickly crusted, one and all:
The rusted nails fell from the knots
   That held the peach to the garden-wall.
The broken sheds look'd sad and strange:
   Unlifted was the clinking latch;
   Weeded and worn the ancient thatch
Upon the lonely moated grange.
     She only said, "My life is dreary,
       He cometh not," she said;
     She said, "I am aweary, aweary,
       I would that I were dead!"

Her tears fell with the dew at even;
   Her tears fell ere the dews were dried;
She could not look at the sweet heaven,
   Either at morn or eventide.
After the flittings of the bats,
   When thickest dark did trance the sky,
   She drew her casement-curtain by,
And glanced athwart the glooming flats.
     She only said, "The night is dreary,
       He cometh not," she said:
     She said, "I am aweary, aweary,
       I would that I were dead!"

Upon the middle of the night,
    Waking she heard the night-fowl crow:
The cock sung out an hour ere light:
    From the dark fen the oxen's low
Came to her: without hope of change,
    In sleep she seem'd to walk forlorn,
    Till cold winds woke the gray-eyed morn
About the lonely moated grange.
    She only said, "The day is dreary,
        He cometh not," she said;
    She said, "I am aweary, aweary,
        I would that I were dead!"

About a stone-cast from the wall
    A sluice with blacken'd waters slept,
And o'er it many, round and small,
    The cluster'd marish-mosses crept.
Hard by a poplar shook alway,
    All silver-green with gnarled bark:
    For leagues no other tree did mark
The level waste, the rounding gray.
    She only said, "My life is dreary,
        He cometh not," she said;
    She said, "I am aweary, aweary,
        I would that I were dead!"

And even when the moon was low,
    And the shrill winds were up and away,
In the white curtain, to and fro,
    She saw the gusty shadow sway.
But when the moon was very low,
    And wild winds bound within their cell,

The shadow of the poplar fell
Upon her bed, across her brow.
 She only said, "The night is dreary,
  He cometh not," she said;
 She said, "I am aweary, aweary,
  I would that I were dead!"

All day within the dreamy house,
 The doors upon their hinges creak'd;
The blue fly sung in the pane; the mouse
 Behind the mouldering wainscot shriek'd,
Or from the crevice peer'd about.
 Old faces glimmer'd thro' the doors,
 Old footsteps trod the upper floors,
Old voices called her from without.
 She only said, "My life is dreary,
  He cometh not," she said;
 She said, "I am aweary, aweary,
  I would that I were dead!"

The sparrow's chirrup on the roof,
 The slow clock ticking, and the sound
Which to the wooing wind aloof
 The poplar made, did all confound
Her sense; but most she loathed the hour
 When the thick-moted sunbeam lay
 Athwart the chambers, and the day
Was sloping toward his western bower.
 Then she said, "I am very dreary,
  He will not come," she said;
 She wept, "I am aweary, aweary,
  Oh God, that I were dead!"

# ALFRED TENNYSON

[From] *The Princess*

"Now sleeps the crimson petal, now the white;
Nor waves the cypress in the palace walk;
Nor winks the gold fin in the porphyry font:
The fire-fly wakens: waken thou with me.

Now droops the milk-white peacock like a ghost,
And like a ghost she glimmers on to me.
Now lies the Earth all Danaë to the stars,
And all thy heart lies open unto me.

Now slides the silent meteor on, and leaves
A shining furrow, as thy thoughts in me.

Now folds the lily all her sweetness up,
And slips into the bosom of the lake:
So fold thyself, my dearest, thou, and slip
Into my bosom and be lost in me."

# ALFRED TENNYSON

## As When a Man

**1**

As when a man, that sails in a balloon,
  Downlooking sees the solid shining ground
Stream from beneath him in the broad blue noon,
  Tilth, hamlet, mead and mound:

**2**

And takes his flags and waves them to the mob,
  That shout below, all faces turned to where
Glows rubylike the far-up crimson globe,
  Filled with a finer air:

**3**

So, lifted high, the Poet at his will
  Lets the great world flit from him, seeing all,
Higher thro' secret splendours mounting still,
  Self-poised, nor fears to fall,

**4**

Hearing apart the echoes of his fame.
  While I spoke thus, the seedsman, Memory,
Sowed my deep-furrowed thought with many a name,
  Whose glory will not die.

# ALFRED TENNYSON

[From] *Maud*

## XVIII

### 1

I have led her home, my love, my only friend.
There is none like her, none.
And never yet so warmly ran my blood
And sweetly, on and on
Calming itself to the long-wish'd-for end,
Full to the banks, close on the promised good.

### 2

None like her, none.
Just now the dry-tongued laurels' pattering talk
Seem'd her light foot along the garden walk,
And shook my heart to think she comes once more;
But even then I heard her close the door,
The gates of Heaven are closed, and she is gone.

### 3

There is none like her, none.
Nor will be when our summers have deceased.
O, art thou sighing for Lebanon
In the long breeze that streams to thy delicious East,
Sighing for Lebanon,
Dark cedar, tho' thy limbs have here increased,

Upon a pastoral slope as fair,
And looking to the South, and fed
With honey'd rain and delicate air,
And haunted by the starry head
Of her whose gentle will has changed my fate,
And made my life a perfumed altar-flame;
And over whom thy darkness must have spread
With such delight as theirs of old, thy great
Forefathers of the thornless garden, there
Shadowing the snow-limb'd Eve from whom she came.


4

Here will I lie, while these long branches sway,
And you fair stars that crown a happy day
Go in and out as if at merry play,
Who am no more so all forlorn,
As when it seem'd far better to be born
To labour and the mattock-harden'd hand,
Than nursed at ease and brought to understand
A sad astrology, the boundless plan
That makes you tyrants in your iron skies,
Cold fires, yet with power to burn and brand
His nothingness into man.


5

But now shine on, and what care I,
Who in this stormy gulf have found a pearl
The countercharm of space and hollow sky,
And do accept my madness, and would die
To save from some slight shame one simple girl.

### 6

Would die; for sullen-seeming Death may give
More life to Love than is or ever was
In our low world, where yet 'tis sweet to live.
Let no one ask me how it came to pass;
It seems that I am happy, that to me
A livelier emerald twinkles in the grass,
A purer sapphire melts into the sea.

### 7

Not die; but live a life of truest breath,
And teach true life to fight with mortal wrongs.
O, why should Love, like men in drinking-songs,
Spice his fair banquet with the dust of death?
Make answer, Maud, my bliss,
Maud made my Maud by that long lover's kiss,
Life of my life, wilt thou not answer this?
"The dusky strand of Death inwoven here
With dear Love's tie, makes Love himself more dear."

### 8

Is that enchanted moan only the swell
Of the long waves that roll in yonder bay?
And hark the clock within, the silver knell
Of twelve sweet hours that past in bridal white,
And died to live, long as my pulses play;
But now by this my love has closed her sight
And given false death her hand, and stol'n away
To dreamful wastes where footless fancies dwell
Among the fragments of the golden day.
May nothing there her maiden grace affright!

Dear heart, I feel with thee the drowsy spell.
My bride to be, my evermore delight,
My own heart's heart and ownest own, farewell;
It is but for a little space I go:
And ye meanwhile far over moor and fell
Beat to the noiseless music of the night!
Has our whole earth gone nearer to the glow
Of your soft splendours that you look so bright?
I have climb'd nearer out of lonely Hell.
Beat, happy stars, timing with things below,
Beat with my heart more blest than heart can tell,
Blest, but for some dark undercurrent woe
That seems to draw—but it shall not be so:
Let all be well, be well.

# EMILY BRONTË

[From] *The Prisoner*

'Still, let my tyrants know, I am not doomed to wear
Year after year in gloom, and desolate despair;
A messenger of Hope comes every night to me,
And offers for short life, eternal liberty.

'He comes with western winds, with evening's wandering
    airs,
With that clear dusk of heaven that brings the thickest
    stars.
Winds take a pensive tone, and stars a tender fire,
And visions rise, and change, that kill me with desire.

'Desire for nothing known in my maturer years,
When Joy grew mad with awe, at counting future tears.
When, if my spirit's sky was full of flashes warm,
I knew not whence they came, from sun or thunderstorm.

'But, first, a hush of peace—a soundless calm descends;
The struggle of distress, and fierce impatience ends;
Mute music soothes my breast—unuttered harmony,
That I could never dream, till Earth was lost to me.

'Then dawns the Invisible; the Unseen its truth reveals,
My outward sense is gone, my inward essence feels;
Its wings are almost free—its home, its harbour found,
Measuring the gulph, it stoops and dares the final bound.

'Oh! dreadful is the check—intense the agony—
When the ear begins to hear, and the eye begins to see;
When the pulse begins to throb, the brain to think again;
The soul to feel the flesh, and the flesh to feel the chain.

'Yet I would lose no sting, would wish no torture less;
The more that anguish racks, the earlier it will bless;
And robed in fire of hell, or bright with heavenly shine,
If it but herald death, the vision is divine!'

EMILY BRONTË

*The Night Wind*

In summer's mellow midnight
   A cloudless moon shone through
Our open parlour window,
   And rose-trees wet with dew.

I sat in silent musing;
   The soft wind waved my hair;
It told me heaven was glorious,
   And sleeping earth was fair.

I needed not its breathing
   To bring such thoughts to me;
But still it whispered lowly,
   How dark the woods will be!

'The thick leaves in my murmur
   Are rustling like a dream,
And all their myriad voices
   Instinct with spirit seem.'

I said, 'Go, gentle singer,
   Thy wooing voice is kind:
But do not think its music
   Has power to reach my mind.

'Play with the scented flower,
  The young tree's supple bough,
And leave my human feelings
  In their own course to flow.'

The wanderer would not heed me;
  Its kiss grew warmer still.
'Oh come!' it sighed so sweetly;
  'I'll win thee 'gainst thy will.

'Were we not friends from childhood?
  Have I not loved thee long?
As long as thou, the solemn night,
  Whose silence wakes my song.

'And when thy heart is resting
  Beneath the church-aisle stone,
I shall have time for mourning,
  And *thou* for being alone.'

# EMILY BRONTË

*Ay—There It Is*

'Ay—there it is! it wakes to-night
  Deep feelings I thought dead;
Strong in the blast—quick gathering light—
  The heart's flame kindles red.

'Now I can tell by thine altered cheek,
  And by thine eyes' full gaze,
And by the words thou scarce dost speak
  How wildly fancy plays.

'Yes—I could swear that glorious wind
  Has swept the world aside,
Has dashed its memory from thy mind
  Like foam-bells from the tide:

'And thou art now a spirit pouring
  Thy presence into all:
The thunder of the tempest's roaring,
  The whisper of its fall:

'An universal influence,
  From thine own influence free;
A principle of life—intense—
  Lost to mortality.

'Thus truly, when that breast is cold,
   Thy prisoned soul shall rise;
The dungeon mingle with the mould—
   The captive with the skies.
Nature's deep being, thine shall hold,
Her spirit all thy spirit fold,
   Her breath absorb thy sighs.
Mortal! though soon life's tale is told,
   Who once lives, never dies!'

# EMILY BRONTË

*Stanzas*

Often rebuked, yet always back returning
  To those first feelings that were born with me,
And leaving busy chase of wealth and learning
  For idle dreams of things which cannot be:

To-day, I will seek not the shadowy region;
  Its unsustaining vastness waxes drear;
And visions rising, legion after legion,
  Bring the unreal world too strangely near.

I'll walk, but not in old heroic traces,
  And not in paths of high morality,
And not among the half-distinguished faces,
  The clouded forms of long-past history.

I'll walk where my own nature would be leading:
  It vexes me to choose another guide:
Where the gray flocks in ferny glens are feeding;
  Where the wild wind blows on the mountain side.

What have those lonely mountains worth revealing?
  More glory and more grief than I can tell:
The earth that wakes *one* human heart to feeling
  Can centre both the worlds of Heaven and Hell.

# EMILY BRONTË

*Last Lines*

No coward soul is mine,
No trembler in the world's storm-troubled sphere:
  I see Heaven's glories shine,
And faith shines equal, arming me from fear.

  O God within my breast,
Almighty, ever-present Deity!
  Life—that in me has rest,
As I—Undying Life—have power in Thee!

  Vain are the thousand creeds
That move men's hearts: unutterably vain;
  Worthless as withered weeds,
Or idlest froth amid the boundless main,

  To waken doubt in one
Holding so fast by thine infinity;
  So surely anchored on
The steadfast rock of immortality.

  With wide-embracing love
Thy Spirit animates eternal years,
  Pervades and broods above,
Changes, sustains, dissolves, creates, and rears.

# EMILY BRONTË

Though earth and man were gone,
And suns and universes ceased to be,
    And Thou were left alone,
Every existence would exist in Thee.

There is not room for Death,
Nor atom that his might could render void:
    Thou—THOU art Being and Breath,
And what THOU art may never be destroyed.

# INDEX

*This index has been arranged alphabetically
by title, first line and Poet*

# INDEX

# INDEX

# INDEX